KAITUHI RĀWHITI TWO

KAITUHI RĀWHITI TWO

Weaving of Words

EAST COAST ANTHOLOGY

Edited by
Gillian Moon
Regina de Wolf-Ngarimu
Christopher McMaster

Tairawhiti Writers' Hub

ISBN: 978-0-473-63033-1 (paperback)
978-0-473-63034-8 (Epub)

Front cover image by John Flatt 'Lighseeker Photography'
Weaving Art from the Michelle Hinekura Kerr Collection - Kairāranga Artist
Cover design by Ezra Whittaker-Powley

Visit us at: www.tairāwhitiwrite.com

Printed in Australia

First Printing, 2022

Ka maumahara tatou ki a Rodney Baker, he tangata ngākau nui, he kaitoikupu, he kaikorero paki. Kei roto i ona tuhinga maha, ka rere ko te aroha me te ora.

In memory of Rodney Baker, a founding contributor to Kaituhi Rāwhiti, poet, storyteller and an outstanding man who imbued his words with emotion and life.

CONTENTS

Introduction

'Tena tātou e te Whānau.
Every anthology is a constellation and, like summer stars, Kaituhi Rāwhiti Two has risen again over the East Coast. It's a thrilling ascent to watch, with last year's editors and writers joined by new contributors in a bigger and more expansive display of Te Tairawhiti mana and literary power. I congratulate the editorial team for their hard work in easing Kaituhi Rawhiti Two above the horizon so that we can, again, see who our literary stars are. There are some powerful voices coming through and quite a few surprises, including some cuzzies and sistahs who are giving me the hint: move over bro.' – Witi Ihimaera

Kaituhi Rāwhiti Two: Weaving of Words contains writing to touch the wairua of everyone. The book includes talented writers and poets from High School students to octagenarians, new to published authors and everything in between. Like the actions of weaving, the work takes you up and down, over and under, as the flax whips in the opposite direction. The texture, colour and pattern of the weave draw the reader into the fabric of our Whenua. In *Kaituhi Rāwhiti Two,* we have woven poetry and prose into a raurau (basket) brimming with talent. *Kaituhi Rāwhiti Two* is an authentic and unique expression of the people of Te Tairawhiti—creative, diverse, grittily honest, humorous and hopeful. Each contributing author has a connection to the East Coast. The writers from our region tread the trail blazed by Witi Ihimaera 50 years ago. It is, therefore, fitting that Witi, who has given us so much encouragement and support, should have the first and last words.

Gillian, Reg & Chris – Editors

This year's anthology is subtitled Weaving Words from the East Coast. The phrase evokes the image of a whakapapa, of a tukutuku being woven with designs that acknowledge the past, consider the present and look forward to the future. I know that readers will be as moved as I am by stories, poems and memoirs that have special meaning for us Coasties. They portray our lives, our stories of who we are, and our dreams of who we could be.' – Witi Ihimaera

The Italian Campaign

Rodney Baker

We're into the European Theatre
It starts at *The Italian Boot,*
An alpine rocky peninsula
This narrow and coastal chute,

Wretched is winter
With blizzard and blinding snow,
There, the frequent rainstorms
That cold and bitterly blow,

Summer's humid heat
Sharp serpent-like roads,
Mountainous, gullied, ravined
With lots of olive groves,

The 28 Māori Battalion – C Company
The cowboys are here!
Re-equipped and reinforced after the desert
Eager to bear their share,

Sinewed, raw-boned and tough
Route marches and trainings demand,
Endorsement of Te Reo by signals
They broadcast divisions commands,

To artillery in salvos whose shells
Crater and bombard the land,
With a grid creeping barrage
Which shields the infantryman

All attend the open-air service
Heard where everyone stands,
The sermon Wi Te Tau delivers:
The Power, The Kingdom
The Glory, The Crucifixion of Jesus
Forgiveness and blessings to all men,

You learn quickly in battle here
To deal with what's directly in front,
Misjudgements are telling and fatal
Mistakes you make only once.

As assaults are fought through the towns
Close quarters and hand-to-hand,
The populous is right there beside you
Here, you need to be sure of your man,

C Company are in these Italian Hamlets,
Fighting an enemy who wants world rule,
Soldiers from Te Tairāwhiti districts
Have a cavalier ability to keep cool,

Billets and bivouacs resting
Respite from the battle line shows,
Laughter and talk amongst them
Camaraderie and mateship that glows,
Cooking, cleaning, ablutions
Weapons rearm, reports,
A summary of killed and wounded
So, the Muktah can bring up support,

A moment to sit, reflection,
As thoughts drift towards home,
Home at Otanga, Mangatuna
To stroll with his family in tow,

Home where the Waiapu River runs
Swift with the melting of snow,
Home to the Whangara Station
To the flats where the spring lambs grow,

But these are all illusions
There are battles to be fought and won,
Such is the lot of the soldier when
They march to the beat of War's drum.

Te Maro

Te Paea Maurirere

I can picture it. How happy my people were, we thrived on nature, on the land, on each other. Until ....

The Kohu was as thick as night, the rocks cold to touch, as if I were fledgeling looking down from the nest. I look out to the sea. In the distance I notice a big wooden nose emerge from the fog, heading closer. What a strange looking waka? Guest? I looked down to my taiaha, I held in my calloused hands.

I shall greet them. I swirled wind with my taiaha, ready to greet them, hei wero ia rātou, to challenge them. I look down into the water and see my reflection, the son of a chief looks back at me.

A young man, but not young enough to be a child, with shoulders as strong as my maunga, eyes like mud, and sun darkened skin. I begin my wero, my movements precise and natural. I turn my head forward then suddenly, Like uira, it hits my skin, burning. The blood of my tīpuna spilled from my chest.

I must fly. I breathe in, stretch out my parirau; but nothing. He stares me down. As if I am a savage too naive to understand the thoughts of his mind. Conflicted and irritated, I am so confused, I stare into the eyes of a kēhua, a man so pale you'd think he was dead, with eyes as blue as the ocean. Standing over me with intimidation, but I am a warrior, I see the fear in his eyes. His kakahu is unfamiliar to my own, they cover nearly every inch of his pale skin.

A strange weapon in his hand, wooden, but shiny, made of strange metal. It was as if I could see to the end of the inside but it was dark, hollow.

I felt helpless, expecting a gust of wind to come and take me away. I lay there, the last bit of hā leaving my lungs, my last thought to my iwi, who are these strange white men? With so little respect for my tikanga? Do they not know a greeting when they see one?

As I take my last breath, I lay there thinking of what these men bring to my land, and what will become of my people. Who will protect them? I see my brothers in the distance, I want to scream, to yell, “run, tungane, warn our people!" but no words escape my lips.

As my wairua leaves my body, I catch one glimpse of my long black hair spread across the ground. I turn and see a face emerge from the fog once again.

The Endeavour.

Flea's Dream

Janine Hamilton-Kells

People call me Flea. Probably because I'm kind of small and annoying, although that's not unusual—most people are smaller now. I'm out of breath as I walk, my chest is tight and my breath clouds in the morning air. The street is eerily quiet, no one is talking and the electric cars move silently. I'm not often up so early, but today is an important day for me. I pat the zipped pocket of my jacket for the umpteenth time. My shoulders loosen slightly when my fingers brush against the reassuring bulk.

Despite the heaviness of my pace, I'm soon at the train station. A Sleeper stands in the growing light wrapped in a brown coat, his face wrinkled and hopeful. He's handing out information about our destination; "Mountain views and clean air," he calls, "euphoria, increased alertness, innovation and creation." He's smiling and nodding as we take the fliers and move into the crowd. People nod benignly, they don't need convincing, my generation anticipates the Alpine Dream Festival like nothing else in our calendar, barring a pandemic, nothing would stop us from attending.

After my first festival, my mood levels had skyrocketed and my thoughts had a buoyancy I had never experienced before. Everything had been so beautiful it seemed my eyes weren't able to adjust when I returned. For the first time, I'd been able to focus on an object or a task and to interact with people successfully face to face—I've been chasing that feeling ever since. There are rumours that there might be natural sunlight this year, but Zeb and I are looking forward to the musicians the most, neither of us has seen live music before. Zeb's talked of nothing else for weeks.

Since my generation lost the ability to sleep, we've lost a lot of things. Our health, our immunity and our ability to procreate. We are also the first generation that can no longer dream. This means it's difficult for us to process emotion, to store memories and to create. There's been no new music, literature or art in two decades. Life is a continuous rerun—an artistic time-warp. I scan the station platform for Zeb, his tall frame and shock of white-blond hair make him easy to spot in a crowd. My hand drifts to my pocket again, patting it like a talisman. I'm shuffling closer to the Perspex partitions that funnel to the train entrance. The queues are orderly. We've spent our child-hood's queuing each day to receive the things required to fill the deficit in our bodies, waiting is one of the rare things we do well.

I close my eyes and shudder at the closeness of all the bodies, my nose wrinkles and my backpack presses against me from the wall of people behind. The couple in my ear are older, a man and a woman, they look like Sleepers but it could just be the chronic insomnia —it ages you. They wear colourful lanyards but I can't read what they say without turning fully. I'm not going to risk this; my clumsiness is legendary--quite a feat in a generation renowned for their lack of coordination.

The woman speaks quietly to her partner.

"Will this work?"

"It has to," he replies. "We've put everything we have into these VIP tickets." Their desperation is so naked and raw I glance away quickly.

"As VIPs we'll get our own dream pod and a personal guide for dreaming meditations, we've done everything they advised," he takes her hand.

"This is our best chance to be parents and if it doesn't work, we'll know we've done everything we possibly could," he speaks with a quiet determination and she attempts a weak smile but her eyes fill and she scrubs tears away with her sleeve.

"We'll have a lamb of our own," she says like a mantra as they are funnelled into a different side of the entrance. I lose their conversation but their exchange leaves me discomforted, as if I've intruded on an intimacy. Most people here are carrying some kind of hope or agenda. I touch my pocket fleetingly. What would it be like to have a little human dependent on you? To have that kind of optimism to believe in a future?

A shout carries across the busy station. I breathe a sigh of relief. Zeb pushes his way through the crowd. "Excuse me, moving on through here, sorry about that." He gives a running commentary of his progress to the obvious annoyance of the other commuters, but nobody stops him. Typical Zeb, I suppress a smile.

"I didn't think you'd make it."

"Of course, I was going to make it, but that was cutting it tight though, even for me." His smile brightens his whole face and I answer it with one of my own. My cheeks are tight.

"This is kind of crazy huh? It's weird seeing so many people out at once." His vintage band t-shirt is tucked into faded jeans, and a worn tartan jacket reaches his knees.

"I was thinking the same thing, it's strange to think of the empty flats and buildings, to think that we will all be together on the mountain with mainly Sleepers, and a few Lambs left behind."

"Yeah, perhaps they can take a collective nap while we are all there saving the future of humankind." Zeb raises an eyebrow then cracks a grin. His teeth flashing white despite his pale skin. I choke on a laugh. Only Zeb could be so flippant about something as sacred as sleeping.

The Dream Festivals are a smorgasbord of poetry, art and music. But I have an agenda. At my first festival, I had an almost perfect moment with Zeb. We had danced together in the moonlight, and I had experienced a moment of joy that seemed to hang suspended like a freeze-frame. After the festival, I searched my tired mind for the memory every morning and each day it dissipated a little more until I could scarcely remember the feeling of my limbs moving, the moon's rays energising my skin, Zeb's crooked smile and the bubble of emotion that lifted me like a thousand pinpricks of light. I searched my mind systematically as if rummaging through dusty boxes in a storage locker. Nothing. All I have is the photograph to prove it happened.

Zeb's lanky frame serves as a barrier against the worst of the pushing and shoving as people cram onto the train. I lean against a railing. I come up to Zeb's bicep on a tall day and his long arm stretches above me as he holds the handrail. I imagine pressing my nose against the soft skin of his underarm, inhaling his scent, his skin soft against my face, his warmth pressed against my nose as I breathe him in. I blink and refocus and look up at Zeb. He picks a piece of thread from my hair.

"I like the new colour," he teases.

"Shut up," I blush. Zeb knows the home colouring went horribly wrong. I'm lucky the burnt orange ends hadn't fallen out completely. I look through the tangle of heads and shoulders and catch a glimpse of the city. The buildings are becoming more spaced apart and the sight soothes me. I stand staring into the grey as the rhythmic motion of the train gently rocks us toward our destination.

"Mel will meet us at the transfer station." Zeb looks out the window as he speaks.

"Cool," The warmth in my gut, diminishes. I glance up at him, he looks down and I glance away. I'm aware of the skin tight over my face and I feel his gaze land on my cheekbone. I look determinedly through the head of a commuter until Zeb shifts his focus away.

Mel is uncomplicated—lovely, with a larger than normal dose of sunny disposition. How she maintains her blatant positivity is beyond me. It's surprising that she hasn't been snapped up for some kind of government study. It's unnatural, and I'm stunned Zeb's fallen for it—depression defines our generation. I put my earphones on and a few moments later Zeb does the same. I'm beginning to feel tired now, the dragging fatigue tugging at me like a lamb pulling on its mother's hem. I remember Mel as a seven-year-old with long curly hair and a gap in her teeth, we had lived in the same building and attended a learning pod together. Zeb was a couple of years older and had exuded a level of unattainable cool even as a gangly teen. Now I see Mel weekly at our hormone and cell renewal therapy. I'm purposely late, securing the last reclining chair by the door. As I lie there with the cocktail of preservatives and chemicals filling my defective body, I try to visualise a healing light entering my bloodstream like the phosphorescence of the sea that I've read about. When the IV bag hangs empty, I rush to be unhooked and gone before Mel can collect her belongings and attempt to catch me.

We shuffle off the train at the station and breathe in the clean air. The anticipation is tangible, people move with a lightness of step, unplugged and talking quietly. The crush of the crowd threatens to separate us and Zeb grabs my hand. His hand is so large and so warm it's like putting mine into a pocket. I close my eyes, willing this memory to imprint in my inefficient brain, *his hand, remember this*. We are swept along ending up on the edges of the crowd like twigs carried along in a current. The throng clears and we both look around for Mel. The crowd parts and there she is. She's wearing a white cap and a yellow scarf. Yellow. Seriously. The white and the yellow and the blonde of her hair make her seem like the only coloured in person on an uncoloured page. Ridiculous.

Zeb lifts his hand, breaking contact with mine and waves to her. Her face lights up and she waves back, positively skipping to join us. I arrange my face into a neutral expression.

"Hey, you two! You're here! It's so great to see you!" I'm sure she is bouncing on her toes and I cast my eyes to her feet to check, but she remains grounded.

"Hey," I say trying to drag her down with the tone of my voice.

"Hey, isn't this epic?" Zeb smiles at Mel. I flex my empty hand.

"Flea, it's been so long, it feels like we never see each other these days." Even her reproach is endearing and she links her hand through my arm joining us in the way that we used to walk everywhere together, our elbows bumping.

"You know how it is," I mumble and despite everything, I feel myself responding to Mel, drawn in to her iridescent wake.

The gravel crunches under our feet as we move to the bus queue together, the chill of the mountain breeze curls around the collar of my jacket. People do a double-take as they see Mel, with all her energy and brightness, the three of us are an odd ensemble. I pull my fried orange hair down lower over my face, my fringe already curling in a thousand wrong directions. The bus ride passes in a blur of excited chatter, the bus is full and I'm in the awkward position of being squashed between Zeb and Mel, Zeb's long arm framing the back of our seat. Mel's chatter is incessant and I zone out. Mum has told me about the days before they knew how dangerous screens were, when people used to sit on public transport their headphones plugged into physical devices. It must have been so peaceful. Of course, nobody had known just what the impact that blue light would have on a generation of developing brains—changing our cells at a molecular level and rendering us unable to sleep. By the time they banned screens, devices and blue light, the damage was done. Now the Sleepers are aging and no way of reversing the damage has been found. The Dream Festivals have become crucial, without the creative thinking that comes when people dream, we may never find a way to reverse the effects on our damaged generation.

I tune back into the conversation floating back and forth. I haven't really observed these two interacting at all, this is our first outing in almost a year. I've actively avoided them since I was body-slammed by the news that they were together. I pat my pocket discreetly and glance at Mel. My cheeks colour and I take a deep breath looking down at my hands.

"You okay Flea?" Zeb's breath is warm on my temple.

"Yep, yep, I'm great," I say, my voice coming out too loudly. I catch them glancing at each other and I cringe.

Zeb reads aloud from our information pack using his best Sir David Attenborough voice, the voice that is used for our public service announcements.

We are a nation that excels in technology, with every generation we have made advancements. But the arts are different. They require a human element, a perfect storm of faith, emotion, angst, frustration, love and fear. These things need to be felt. We are willing to invest whatever it takes to create the right environment for dreaming. The results we hope for could provide the solutions we need in today's world. The hopes of all humankind are pinned on you, our future dreamers.

We've heard it all before but still, Mel hangs on to every word her eyes shining. "I can't wait," she smiles. "All of the new beginnings, the music and there's always romance at the festivals."

"Yeah, but it does it last?" Zeb and I say in perfect synch. We laugh holding each other's eyes for a millisecond.

"Although in Gen ZZZ years, relationships are twice as long--sleepers spend half their relationships sleeping after all," remarks Zeb and I smirk with him. Tugging down Mel's blatant positivity is an art form.

"Imagine sleeping next to someone though, it must be so intimate, the trust, the abandon of it." Mel clutches her hands to her chest. She's like some kind of witch I think—impossible to hate. I try to imagine her with a disfiguring disease marring her golden features. It doesn't help and suddenly it's all too much.

I leap up and push Zeb's knee back down when he tries to stand with me. "Just stay. I need some air. I feel sick." I stumble down the aisle.

"Can I do anything?" Mel's sweet voice floats behind me in concern. *Just die,* I think, then shame floods through me instantly. *Arggh this was always going to be the shittest idea. I'm a despicable person.*

I don't deserve him.

I stay seated at the front of the bus until we arrive. The views during the ascent are magnificent but still, I find my eyelids growing heavy and my eyes unable to focus. I pop a caffeine pill to keep me functioning for a while longer, gathering my backpack and moving off the bus. Zeb and Mel materialise at my shoulder.

"Right," I say brightly, determined to soldier on as if I hadn't humiliated myself. "Where to next?"

"Let's find our pod," beams Mel and strides off. Zeb smiles at me and shrugs. I turn and follow.

As we move through the entrance, the mountains encircle us as if they are a great pair of healing hands rising from the earth and holding us to the sun. Objects are keenly outlined and coloured vividly and actual birdsong fills the air. I glance at Mel who is spinning, her arms outstretched in rapture, she's like a colourful bird. I glance at my heavy boots to keep myself from smiling, she's infectious, the corners of my mouth keep tugging up against gravity.

A vibration moves through my boots, travelling up my skinny legs and filling my belly. Music like I've never heard before drifts up the valley. A slow smile spreads across Zeb's face and he turns to me. Our eyes lock. All around us people look in wonder, taking in the grandeur. The collective mood-lifts like air bubbles fizzing to the surface of a drink, I visualise them popping, my nose wrinkling with delight and my eyes watering. I tilt my head back, willing this moment to permeate me. I think of the photograph in my pocket. *Please work.*

The mood is broken by guides directing us to our pods, I enter, throwing my backpack on the chair nearest the door and we pause for a moment unused to making decisions in this trio.

"We should eat." Zeb looks at his info sheet again. "Picnic in the sunshine anyone?"

"You two go on ahead," says Mel. "I want to get changed; I'll find you." I leave the pod without a backwards glance, casting a wave over my shoulder. Zeb follows closely behind. A rightness settles between us.

We move through the valley, soft grass springy under our feet, Zeb collects a wicker picnic basket from a stand. It contains a soft blanket, freshly made food, and a bottle of sparkling wine.

"We may already be dreaming," I sigh.

"Seems like it." His grin is easy and natural.

We settle on a patch of grass not far from the other picnic goers but far enough to create an illusion of privacy. Anxiety churns in my stomach, the scene feels fraudulent as if I'm stealing someone else's moment. Zeb lies back on his tartan coat, his pale arms stretched above, cushioning his head in his hands. I sit awkwardly, my arms wrapped around my bony knees.

"Are you hungry?" I ask.

"Not particularly, but thirsty yes." I pour drinks, leaving Mel's glass in the basket and closing the lid with a snap. The crispness of the wine is sharp on my tongue. Zeb is still lying back propped on one elbow, he nudges me.

"Happy?"

"Yes," I say simply, with shaky hands I reach into my pocket fumbling with the button.

"This is gorgeous!" exclaims Mel. My hand freezes, my heart plummets as she flings herself onto our blanket. Zeb looks away. I lay back, plug my headphones into my ears, and shut them out with my eyelids.

Later a lineup of musicians carries the crowd toward the collective dreaming, anticipation building as the evening unfolds. Mel suggests we walk to the pod together to get warmer clothes and I acquiesce. Zeb stands mesmerised by the musicians on stage and he waves us off with a grin.

The pod is cosy, no sound comes through the walls. It's intimate--almost womblike.

"It's so nice to be here with you Flea, I've missed you." I make a noncommittal sound, my back turned toward her as I rifle through my backpack.

"Flea, can I ask you something?" My heart stills and I nod but continue to sort through my clothes. "Have I done something wrong? Something to damage our friendship?"

I open my mouth to refute it but stop, taking a deep breath.

"It's just a little awkward with you and Zeb now," I manage.

"But why? I don't understand." A rare frown crosses Mel's face like a cloud across the sun.

"Being together, it's weird." I turn away from her, my cheeks burning.

"We're not together."

I throw her a filthy look loaded with hurt, betrayal and layered with disbelief.

"We're not."

"Look, Wez told me you got together last summer after the festival."

"And you believed him? Is that why you've been avoiding me all these months? You haven't been avoiding Zeb!"

"You knew how I felt about him." My voice is dead like a cloth wrung out.

"We're not together Flea, we never were." Mel's voice weaves its way into my head. "We had one weird night when we got a little drunk and ended up talking all night about our lost loves and that's it." She sighs. "Open your eyes Flea, he's into you."

The room tilts and I sit on the bed. My mind running over the last ten months frantically rearranging them in a new light. I remember the photo in my pocket and a flush creeps over my skin.

"Flea? Something's been bugging me." Mel moves toward me tentatively. "Did you take that photo I had of you and Zeb together? The one I showed you at therapy?"

My cheeks flame.

"Yes," I rub my hand over my face, unable to look at her. "I thought if I brought it here and showed him during the festival he might remember it, that moment—remember me even."

"Oh, Flea."

"I'm sorry," my voice is small as if the magnitude of the mountains and Mel's disappointment in me is bearing down on it. Long excruciating moments pass.

"I guess we're going to need a plan then," Mel says, I look up in surprise and she grins. I move closer to her as if I could soak up some of her golden light.

"I've missed you," I say and my heart eases, a year of hurts melting.

We return to the basin, Zeb waves out to us and we make our way over. I take him in. All these months have passed, why didn't I just ask him? I look at Mel for a moment and I know the answer. Because I thought there was no way he would want me when he could have Mel. Who wouldn't choose Mel? Sleepers move through the crowd handing out the monitor stickers and sealed drinks that are essential for the REM sleep preparations. I look up at Zeb. He's more alive here in this place, his dark eyes shining in the dusk, his lanky frame assured in his movements. There's a coolness about him which is hard to describe. Like Mel, he stands out, how did I end up with these two? How does someone like me fit?

Nerves flutter in my throat as the time for the dreaming draws closer, Mel keeps flashing secret smiles at me and as much as I try it's harder and harder to meet them with my sarcastic eye-rolls.

"What?" says Zeb when he intercepts one.

"Nothing," I say quickly. "Mel is just being Mel." He smiles at this looking between Mel and I. I know he can sense there's been a shift between us.

Thick thermal blankets have been laid out on the grass. People drift toward them ready to begin the mass dreaming that has drawn us to this ephemeral place. We find a spot halfway from the stage, sinking into the warm blanket. Mel scoots to the edge so that I am between them both, delivering meaningful looks that are so weighted her head nods with them. We uncap our drinks at the suggestion of the MC and I hold mine up.

"Here's to us, and dreaming," I say.

"To us," answers Zeb.

"To romance and dreams come true," smiles Mel. I shoot her a glance and she laughs, tipping her head back and sculling her drink.

Zeb and I drink ours more leisurely, and as I lower my bottle Zeb reaches his hand up and brushes away a little of the drink from the corner of my lip with his thumb. I blush and he grins.

"I have something," I say quickly as the drink begins to take effect, the guided meditation starts to filter through the basin into our primed ears. The lights are dimmed and people hunker down to look up at the stars.

"Yes?" Zeb's voice is thickening.

"I wanted to show you this." I open my pocket and pull out the photo. It has captured us in a moment, spinning in the moonlight, our arms embracing each other, our faces tilted toward one another, paused on the precipice of something.

"Oh Flea," Zeb's voice is hoarse. "I have one too." He reaches into the back pocket of his jeans and pulls out an identical photo, even more worn and dog-eared than my own.

"How?" I say.

"Mel gave it to me, she printed a copy for both of us, to help us remember. I thought you'd forgotten."

"Mel?" I turn.

"Just pretend I'm not here," she says, eyes closed and lying beneath the stars. "You two have wasted enough time already."

Zeb grins, his teeth white in the dimming light, he reaches for me pulling me into the depths of his tartan coat. I cup his lovely face with both of my hands kissing him before the pull of the drug-induced sleep tugs us down onto the blanket next to Mel. It's the closest thing to happiness I've ever known.

His hand is in mine as we stand overlooking the majestic valley, the people dreaming peacefully stretched out below us. Beautiful images, musical notes, and colours are swirling above their heads like a whirlpool of exquisite energy. I'm filling with light, the imperfect and defective me, the awkwardness of my person, my movements, my clumsy thoughts--none of it matters. For some incomprehensible reason, it hasn't scared Zeb away. He looks at me as if I'm whole. I raise my head and a current of light, hope and heat flows between us before we jump into the perfect storm below.

East Coast Gothic

Aaron Compton

Cherry tomatoes
are sweeter, tastier,
having hung in the Tairāwhiti sun
for a fortnight on a dead vine.

Making Overtures to Hine Raukatauri

Aaron Compton

For too long no man has made you gasp.
I know I could make you *sing*,
given the chance,
but you, always on display yet
always unattainable,
mouth open and breathless,
you lie on your non-volatile pillow,
behind glass,
the sockets of your once blue iridescent eyes
now staring blankly,
your stone-carved lips
dry.

I long
to give my mouth to your open mouth,
I long
to give my breath to your song,
putōrino.

Sprung

Aaron Compton

my world turns,
wobbling like a spinning top.
the first day of spring falls
eight days before my birthday but
the ebb and flow of sap pays heed to no calendar,
responds to no meeting requests,
so I must go find it in her:
my world.

I track her spoor,
a boot print,
trowelled earth,
a trail of empty bean pods,
laughter.

seven days fade in and out,
from and to black,
lost and found and lost again

until

fuzzy buds,
until
sweating dawn dew,
until
swelling stems
embossed with branching traceries of life,
leaves backlit like stained church glass,
telling the story of a god being born again
and again
every morning it rises anew—

and here she is,
Nature incarnate Herself,
wearing no watch and little else but
dialling
a relative angle to the sun,
striking
a spark
to twinkle in her eye
and

I watch
the time draw near
as her shadow shrinks,

my *kāheru* ready in hand,
I wait,
for the not-so-shy creature to approach;

in vain.
the dark night of the soul
becomes dawn once more

before I realise my fear has become excitement:
that 5am gut flutter,
that feeling
like the first day of the school holidays,
memories of the crunch and astringency of green plums,
a rush of saliva,
the seasons turning under the blankets.

I hear her soft chuckle in the dim light of my camp.
I roll over with a smile; she's found me,
sprung.

Re-mind

Aaron Compton

It wasn't destined that you,
young lady, would hear him, a young man,
whistling pretty outside your window.
You were not obliged,
having heard his melody,
to step out with him.
Having stepped out together
you weren't fated to make contracts
and co-sign papers for fifty years.
After sharing a half century of certain tax returns
it wasn't long
before that *other* certainty
closed his curtains.

I don't want you to forget
who you are to me
but your stories are slipping away so
I'll record them and play them back to you,
your own voice re-minding yourself.

We'll play some Louis, some Ella too,
it was always about the jazz with you two,
no one in town could blow a horn
ALL the way around a tune
like your man— like my Pa—
that's a third certainty, eh Ma?

Sweet Treat

Norman McClean

It's not every day that a Queen comes to town, as everyone who set foot in the shop observed when they dropped in to buy custard squares and Afghan biscuits. The screen door clicked open, and the tinkling bell above it could have been a baby brother of Big Ben—it really could—as Ngaire thought one morning, leaning into the window space with a Fielder's sponge plumply risen and finely dusted with icing sugar.

A royal visit demanded something of an effort. Every shop in town was being draped in patriotic bunting while at the War Memorial near the garage there was a kind of steel arch erected with lights along its edges that lit up after sunset as if She was already here, having a cuppa somewhere, perhaps, her white high-heels slipped off in the heat and Philip with loosened tie, lolling in a comfy chair, worn out after all that hand shaking.

Ngaire strung red, white and blue pennants across the inside of the window, their little sharp ends pointing down at the cupcakes and the chocolate eclairs on their silver stands. The whole place became a veritable parlour of loyal delights as she explained to Basil that night, rubbing in cold cream and feeling a wiggle of excitement at the thought there were only a few days to go. Basil didn't go much on all the fuss. He hardly glanced up from his book. She glanced at him in the mirror and wished he wouldn't do up the top button on his pyjamas. He looked like someone's granddad.

Each afternoon ogling kiddies on their way home after summer holiday high jinks pressed their faces to the window, smearing the glass with damp lip marks and tiny fragments of half-sucked sherbet. There were little paw prints everywhere that set Ngaire scuttling out with a damp rag after the last of them had drifted away, craving what a few pennies could not provide.

Not that all the kids cared that much about the Queen as she explained to Basil that night. They might parade around with those school issued imitation gold medals suspended from a little blue tag pinned to their jerseys but really ... The boys scoffed at their sisters' scrap-books full of photos clipped from magazines and made as their focus the royal train or that bloody big ship that everyone called the *Royal Yacht.*

She'd hear their prattle when they paused to drool over lamingtons stuffed with wedges of mock cream and Belgian biscuits speckled with hundreds and thousands. Their Mums went past with baskets on their arms or leaning on their pushchairs and if they popped in to pick up something special before the weekend, it was their mounting excitement that made them sometimes over-spend.

"Good thing so many of them are too lazy to fill their own tins," Basil said. "Business is booming, girl!" He forked up a chunk of dumpling with his mince and gave a satisfied wiggle. "You're a dab hand with the finishing touches, I'll say that."

Before he went off to the Bank in the morning, he watched her flicking a tea towel at a couple of hovering flies. "There are fly specks on the pennants already," Ngaire complained. "We really need a fly-screen here, on the inside of the window instead of this stupid sliding glass door. I don't want my baking spoiled."

Basil said he'd see to it sometime which meant he'd forget about it until the visit was over and all the fuss with it. Ngaire remembered a helpful young chap at Barker's who went out of his way that time to fix broken boards on the back veranda. When she gave the place a ring, it was the young man himself who answered. Could he, she wondered, knock up a flyscreen for the window?

No problem, he said. If she could let him have the exact measurements, he could have it done in a couple of days. A small difficulty there, Ngairie explained; she wasn't at all sure that they actually owned a tape measure. Could he possibly pop around about closing time if it wasn't out of his way? Basil had to work late unfortunately but she would be home.

The Barker's bloke said it'd be as good as gold—he'd see her soon after five.

And if looking hard means seeing, he saw her. She could see that much for herself. From the moment he leaned his bike against the lamp post and swung through the door with a tape measure in his hand, his cheery grin and direct stare made her think of an Alsatian dog, all white teeth and a kind of gentle panting. Not much was said while he ran the extending length of flexible tape around the inside of the window but when she pressed him to a date scone—they hadn't all sold that morning—he winked when he bit into it and said it was the best damned scone he'd eaten in ages.

Ngaire started to blather a bit—Basil was always telling her about it—so she made a cuppa, watched the Barker's bloke stir in a scoop of sugar, stir it as if his life depended on it then down it in a few swallows. It was only when he leaned on the counter with a stub of pencil to enter in his notebook a couple of calculations and asked what a pretty woman like her was doing in a two-bit cake shop, that she thought she really ought to assert herself.

"Two bits?" Ngaire queried, remembering the gangster films that Basil enjoyed so much when they went to the Roxy of a Saturday. "Don't you mean, two bites?"

"Two bites," he murmured. "Yeah, that'd be nice, eh?"

She gave a small involuntary giggle and buried her nose in her own cup while the pencil went click, click on the wooden counter and he slowly pushed his mug forward asking if there was any chance of another. Ngaire contemplated offering him a Melting Moment as well but instead dithered her way back to the kitchenette then did something unnecessary at the cash register while he was sipping his second lot, more slowly this time and saying he'd bring the screen round on Friday if that'd suit. She saw how he wiped his mouth with the back of his hand, a very faint trail of steam still rising from his tea.

Feeling more in charge now, she asked his name. Joe Carlson it was with a warm hand-shake and she was …? He cocked an eyebrow at her name, said you didn't hear Ngaire, too often, did you? She disregarded that and assured him that Friday would be wonderful if he could manage it. Joe flicked back his Brylcreamed cowlick and still grinning said he could manage most things.

She saw him out, bolted the front door, turned the sign to Closed and stared at the flies performing Latin American dances over the now empty cake stands while others were settling for the night in her dangling thicket of Union Jacks. Basil would not be best pleased at the cost of the new screen, but it was ordered now and really, you couldn't risk even a single fly being seen behind the glass—not with the Royal Visit on and everything.

Surprisingly, Basil didn't make a fuss about it at all: long term improvements are long term investments Basil opined over their corned beef that evening.

There was something about long term investments that stuck in Ngaire's head, she just couldn't say why. She found the words popping up even when she rolled out pastry and piped pink icing around the top of an ordered birthday cake. An improvement being like something you got only by investing made her wonder if sticking her small savings through the slot in her moneybox, a gift from someone when she turned ten, would improve things long term. It really was time she stopped that kiddy nonsense and started popping into the Post Office more regularly so that she could experience that small thrill of satisfaction at her savings growing each time the teller tallied them up and thumped his stamp over the neatly penned numbers.

When Basil went off to work on Friday, there was a little flutter under Ngaire's apron that made her prattle in a specially bright and cheery manner to every single customer and twice she dropped a pie before sliding it into a brown paper bag. Basil had been asked to drive out by the orchards before coming home to buy plums and peaches: she really had to start preserving and it would only take him a short time after work, wouldn't it? Using tinned fruit in her luscious flans and tarts was something she only ever did in an emergency like if she'd forgotten to simmer the slices in their syrup for a while before adding spices.

As she turned the sign to Closed shortly before five o'clock, she noticed a kiddy outside the window, digging a small wooden spatula into his little carton of Frosty Jack ice cream. She wished he'd go away: Joe Carlson with a screen under one arm could be appearing any minute now.

"Gidday Joe Carlson!" The child's high piping came through the glass. "Shops' shut —you've missed out."

"P'rhaps not," Joe said, swinging one leg over the bar. He ruffled the kid's hair. "On your way home? Good boy—your Mum will be wondering where you are."

His rap on the door made Ngaire almost trip on a chair as she bustled to the door, reached up to unbolt it. "Goodness, I'd almost forgotten you were coming!" she said. "Oh, what a lovely screen, Joe. It's perfect."

"Perfect if it fits right," Joe said. "Let's see if I 'm going to be able to get it in without a struggle."

"My husband's not in," Ngaire said," or we could pay you now. He looks after that side of things."

"When the cat's away," Joe Carlson said easily, shoving his stub of yellow pencil behind one ear. "I'll send an account. Meanwhile I'd happily settle for a Ginger Kiss. Now, could I get you to hold up the other end of this glass thing? Nice and steady now, I need to get it up gently."

He unscrewed the glass panel, gave it to her to put aside while he carefully slotted the screen into ready grooves. She watched him leaning and half crouching, came close when he called for a hand to support one corner. With sleeves rolled up and his brown arms lifting, Joe's sweat gave off a sweet scent that made her think of old apples in a wooden box. He whistled between his teeth and made bird noises through pursed lips. With a final jerk and a gentle shove, it was clear that the screen fitted snugly. Ngaire laughed in delight, slid it back and forth several times for the sheer pleasure of seeing how smoothly it glided, how completely it would prevent a single fly from penetrating the sacred sanctum beyond.

Together they faced the footpath. Miss Jamieson from the Public Library strolled past, gave a small wave, her eyes flicking over the unfamiliar male figure behind the realm that held sweet treats for all in need, registering—Ngaire knew it in a flash—that Basil was not there to help with this after-hours procedure.

"Who needs the Queen, eh?" Joe said as she went off to make him a cup of tea. "Give me a princess any day."

Ngaire popped a Ginger Kiss on a plate and handed him his mug, ready sugared. "Fresh today," she said, wondering why her voice gave that little wobble. "I think you might like it."

"I know I will," Joe said. He nibbled slowly, crumbs tumbling from his lips to fall down his shirt front, half opened—oh, purely by chance—to show his sun-tanned chest. "Where's the husband this afternoon then?"

She explained about peaches and preserving, rattled on about the busy life of baking for a demanding public. Curiously, Joe expressed an interest in commercial sized ovens. What could be more natural than her bright offer to show him out the back, only if he could be bothered—if he liked.

Oh, he did, that became very evident.

Joe twiddled with switches, crouched to peer into cavernous spaces from which issued each morning another range of temptations. The scent of yeast, he exclaimed—it was everywhere. He inhaled like a man gasping for air, grinned at her in the half light of the bakery and started talking about what hard work it must be, all that rolling and pressing. It made her clench her fists against her apron pocket.

"I expect you'll need to be getting on," Ngaire said. "Someone will have dinner on the go, won't they?"

Joe shook his head slowly. "Nah, I rent a little place over near the river. Get my own grub but it's nothing fancy, I can tell you. I eat when I feel like it." He picked up a couple of currants with the tip of one finger, put them on his tongue. "Sweet, that's a fact. Taste."

Before she could refuse, he was bringing one finger up to her mouth, gently inserting one of the tiny black specks of sweetness. Ngaire blinked rapidly but swallowed then found herself suddenly a little out of breath. The bakery was always warm, but she felt she should be pushing open a window and to hell with the flies. Perhaps she should switch on the fan. Joe had reached out one arm and quite deliberately run his hand over her own where it gripped the edge of the roll-out bench. Which is how she came to find herself leaning back on the still floury table-top, her spine arching, while he came slowly closer still, talking in the back of his throat about the mouth-watering scent of yeast and of, you know, buns in the oven.

When he lifted one hand, quite gently, to brush a trace of flour from her hair, she could only swallow hard and found she just didn't want to stop him.

The metallic snake belt that held up his jeans gave a clink as it loosened.

Basil remarked that she was particularly quiet that evening.

Well, it was Friday after all, and it had been a thoroughly tiring week, hadn't it? There were plums to deal with next morning—she really needed an early night and no, Basil might just as well sit up listening to the wireless if he wanted to, as really, she was just so exhausted.

Lying in her bath she thought of the day as being something like the sort of dream she might have had at high school or something she'd half hoped might be seen rather than merely hinted at in the pictures on some distant Saturday night. It was only when hanging up her towel that she discovered by glancing in the half-fogged mirror, a peculiar, indented pattern on one shoulder. She rubbed the mirror almost clear, twisted her neck and realised with a little jolt that it was from the slit in the top of the roll-out bench.

Dough for pastries, Ngaire thought, pastries for tarts. She threw up in the toilet and shivering with shock, clutched her summer dressing gown around her as she huddled her way to bed, not even bothering to turn on the light. The warmth of the January evening didn't do a thing to stop the way she trembled, staring at the fanlight above the window where the shadow of the kowhai tree threw tentative fingers in her direction.

The following evening, just as she was reaching into the window to adjust the cardboard image of Elizabeth and Philip on their wedding day, there was Joe Carlson. No bike this time, he was on foot and giving her a rapid wink as he strolled past in stove-pipe trousers, motorbike boots and despite the summer warmth, a leather jacket with a lambswool collar; a perfect hood in an American movie. His hair was creamed and combed with Presley precision. Across the road, outside the Mayfair Dairy where the motorbike boys congregated on Saturday evenings, someone gave a piercing whistle. Joe swaggered across to join his mates.

They are like kids, Ngaire thought—well, a lot of them are little more really. And how old can *he* be—eighteen, nineteen? With legs crossed the young bloods lolled against the Mayfair's wall with jutting backsides and hands dug deep in pockets so that their elbows crooked. They whistled and called out to passing girls, wagging their heads when they raucously laughed and blowing smoke rings as if their lives depended on it.

You're twenty-nine, Ngaire Parsons, and you're married, she thought. *Twenty-nine,* and he's a kid. She turned away so abruptly she barked one shin against the counter and gave a yelp of pain.

"Problem, dear?" Basil inquired coming in from the back.

"It's those young hooligans again," Ngaire said, "cluttering up the footpath and making a nuisance of themselves." She made room for Basil to join her, and they peered out at the spill of light from the lamp above the Mayfair Café. "Bodgies and so on."

Basil pointed a cautious finger. "There's that smart Alec young beggar from Barker's. Out of control, he is."

Ngaire felt warmth on her throat and her face. "Oh, really? He's the bloke who fitted the new screen. He did rather a good job, I thought." Her mouth went dry. "What's he done to make himself such a bad egg?"

Basil drew her away from the flyscreen. "I'm told no girl's safe around that young larrikin. They say he tries it on with anyone at all. Ought to be seen to."

That would be something of a pity, Ngaire thought; no, that would be going altogether too far. A crime against nature really, when you thought about it. Self-control is no bad thing but nothing more radical, more final, would Joe Carlson need. As for herself, that indented pattern on her shoulder had faded to nothing; it was like having your cake one day and when it's eaten, it's gone. She went with Basil out the back, locked the door to the bakery and settled into their small living room with its contentedly ticking clock and its framed picture over the mantlepiece of The Laughing Cavalier whose eyes she tended to avoid all evening.

There was a kind of frenzy in her baking after that. She produced greater than ever quantities of cream puffs and flaking sausage rolls and jam sponges and Lamingtons. The window was a treasury of delectably tempting treats that emptied throughout the day and kept the cash register ringing happily until closing time. When the bell above the door had jingled for the last time and she had shot the bolt in, it was time to swat those flies that buzzed in gentle frustration against the barrier of that screen, keeping them from the sweet- scented interior of the window space.

Basil was so delighted with business he didn't bother at all with pyjamas one night. Ngaire played her accustomed part well enough, and they talked of how good it would be to have a child although it occurred to her that they seemed to have been trying until they were blue in the face and even after six years of marriage, there had been no encouraging signs at all.

It might have been the Second Coming, so intense was the excitement, the piercing shrieks of rapture when the Queen's car came slowly down their street. Ngaire and Basil stood at the edge of the footpath to wave their Union Jacks and cheer themselves hoarse along with the entire population. In passing, the Duke seemed to smile in the direction of the cake shop where his face as a groom loomed above the jam rolls—Basil got a snap of the real man with his hand raised in greeting—and when the glorious day was over and the crowds had ceased to marvel at the wonder of it all and taken themselves home, Ngaire decided to leave her bunting just where it was, at least until the royal couple had left the country. Anything less seemed almost, well, disloyal.

Exhausted by the exhilaration of the day she bit into a left-over coconut biscuit and leaned against the pastry table, fingering that crack in the wood while Basil went off to have a word with the butcher next door about the amount of gristle in the mince they used to fill pies.

Sweet fragments filled Ngaire's mouth with saliva and such a wave of longing swept over her that she could have dropped her head to that split in the warm wood and just bawled her heart out the way she used to do at the pictures when true love had failed yet again to run smooth. Traces of coconut on her tongue made her suddenly faintly nauseous but that was just silly, quite *impossible* after such a short time. Everything she'd read in those two books from the library that they kept in a locked cupboard, told her it couldn't happen, not so soon. But, oh God, what if ...?

She tried to imagine herself living in some run-down bit of a place near the river with a teen-aged boy's leather boots in the kitchen and on Saturday nights, an empty chair opposite her own. Could she live without her commercial oven and the bins full of flour, sugar? Without Basil, come to that?

She filled a glass from the tap, swirled a strand or two of desiccated coconut from between her teeth and swallowed deeply. There were a few fallen currants on a baking tray yet to be washed. She picked them up one by one, chewed on them reflectively.

They had a sweetness that was like nothing else.

Awaken

Jessica Keast

Morning returns, a sweet-sounding whisper
I hope for gentle warmth as I wake
I beg for happy oblivion
To bask brightly in delight, a gift I believe in

The truth unravels in creeping murmur
I feel the cool blanket of despair
Exhausted from my own theatrics
The brutal mentality of melancholic fear

What is my worth and what is my measure
The mind wanders, the mind worries
The day collides, it splits, it shatters
And still I return to each breath

The truth seems plentiful in telling such lies
Move slowly through the shifting times
I beg forgiveness, for sweetness and nurture
Let me be restful, let me feel pleasure

I can take my own hand, and lead my own way
The tide rises within me, is it hoping, is it willing
The actual core truth of my being
I choose love, shining bright, glowing, beaming

The New Zealand Dream

Sheila

The New Zealand Dream series (*The Seeds are Sown? Growth and Destruction*, and *The Healing*) is an account of Elise's life. It is a journey from birth, growing up in a beautiful country town, moving to the suburbs, and discovering New Zealand's underground. It is a story of survival. In *The New Zealand Dream* trilogy, you will meet characters you may relate to and characters that will shock you. This excerpt is from book two. After Elise's mother and father passed away, she had no one to turn to when her health was failing. She believed her abusive ex-partner and his mother when they said they would help. On this night, Elise learned the only person who could save her was herself. Elise Smith writes under the pen name, Sheila.

The doctor called me in instantly and announced I had two extensive chronic blood clots in my right leg. The contraceptive pills I had been taking were thought to be the cause and my weight. He got the nurse to administer injections straight away to thin my blood. I was to have these every day. The nurse gave me compression stockings to wear. These would help prevent the clots from moving. I was told to go straight to bed and put my legs up high. At any stage these clots could move to my lungs, organs, or brain, killing me instantly. I was warned.

I was put on some super strong painkillers to take once I got home. I still managed to drive home and did what I was told. Now I was confined to bed, I could not work, I could not cook and look after the kids or the house, and I sank into a deep depressive hole once again.

My daughter Bella went to her fathers for the Christmas holidays, his once-a-year gesture. I had no choice but to accept Alister (my son Conor's father) and his mother's offer of coming to stay and help out with the kids. This went okay for a few days until one evening. I had been stuck in bed in my bedroom for days, only able to get to the toilet and painfully wash myself at the bathroom sink. I thought it would be nice to have some company and slowly entered the lounge. I lay on the couch.

The sports news was blaring loudly. I had not seen any of the TV shows I enjoyed for days. I flipped the channel to one of my favourite shows, *Neighbours*, an Australian drama.

'Who changed the channel?' Alister's mother bellowed from the dining room.

'What do you think you are doing?' Alister yelled at me.

'I'd like to watch this, the news is finished,' I replied.

'No, it bloody well is not!' his mother screamed back.

I dug my heels in. This high and mighty queen thought she owned the place. Alister and I were arguing and yelling, his mother joined in. Both were verbally attacking me harshly. I got angry and stood my ground. This was my house and I was not about to tolerate being disrespected again, not in my own home!

Alister's mother began to compare me to my dead mother, putting her down, claiming I was like her, and calling my mother names! The nasty hag had never even sat and had a drink with my mother before. She did not know her one bit! The words she spat were all aimed to tear me down as weak as I already was. She knew what could break me and went in for the kill.

Her demeaning, insulting words hit the air. Something snapped, something deep inside me. I saw red! My hands shook. I heaved my aching body from the couch. I stared at her sitting at my dining room table, smoking cigarettes. Complete and utter rage exploded from deep in my belly. I do not know where I got the strength from. Everything slowed down like a slow-motion movie. I lost control.

I scanned the room for anything I could throw at her. I wanted her to hurt like she had hurt me. I wanted her to feel the pain she so lavishly dished out! I grabbed the ashtray in front of her and hurled it straight at her head. The force was so intense it sped through the air, wiped through her hair on the top of her head, and embedded into the wall above her, missing her by millimetres!

Seeing this sent Alister into a spin. He was roaring at me so loudly. All I could hear were swear words.

'Get the Fuck out my house, leave!" I yelled.

I kept on telling them to leave, but they refused. I grabbed the telephone. 'Get out or I'll call the police!' I screamed at them.

Alister sped towards me. I dragged myself down the hall as fast as I could. I could lock myself in my bedroom till the police arrived. He was too quick. I collapsed on my bed, my legs giving out with intense pain.

Like a flash, he was on me, holding me down. He dug his knee into my legs, pushing all his weight against me. I was alarmed and aware this could encourage the blood clots to move. I was in critical danger! He was still screaming at me. His mother was in the room watching him, egging him on and yelling abuse at me.

I caught a glimpse of Conor by the bedroom door. He was crying and telling them to stop. He vomited on the carpet. I tried with all my strength to push Alister off me to get free. The pain increased.

Tears streamed down my face, blinding my vision. He grabbed my throat with both hands, squeezing the life out of me. Holy shit! He was going to kill me! I wriggled under his weight. He held my arms above my head, pinning me with one arm while he continued to squeeze my neck harder and harder. Fear filled me, the air in my lungs left my body, and my eyes rolled back into my head. All I could hear now was a sharp ringing noise in my head.

Pictures flew through my mind, memories, Bella's birth, Conor's birth, my mother. This cannot be the end! He was not about to stop until I was done. I stopped moving, became still. With the little air I had left in my lungs, I held my breath and closed my eyes. Yes, thank God it worked. He thought I was dead. He stopped, took his hands off my neck, and stood.

As soon as he did, I gathered all the strength I could muster and booted him hard in the knee. This threw him off balance. He stumbled backwards. I screamed as loudly as I could this time, wanting the neighbours to call the police! I leapt to my feet, kneed him in the groin, and scrambled out of the room. Grabbing Conor along the way, I stumbled outside to the letterbox. There under the street lights, in front of the whole street, I knew he would not follow. Anyone could be watching. I used the cordless telephone I'd snatched on the way out and rang the police.

The police arrived soon after. They took statements, they did not ask me if I wanted to press charges, neither were they forthcoming with any information as to how I could protect myself from Alister. I was so exhausted I could barely move. They took Alister and his mother away in the police car, not to the police station to lock them away where they belonged, but a free ride back to his mother's house.

I watched as the police led them both down the driveway. Alister's mother tried to convince the police that Conor did not want to stay with me as she left.

'You don't want to be with her, do you, Conor?' she yelled.

The police knew better. They were not about to let a son be taken away from his mother.

They had not long left. Tears stained my cheeks, and bruises covered my neck. When Bella arrived from her holiday with her dad, I covered up as best as I could and filled her father in on some of the events that had taken place. Of course, he was of little help. He did agree to take Bella for a while longer.

In between drug-induced sleep the next day, I organised Conor to go and stay with my brother Peter. The bills were piling up. I had no way to pay them, and the stress grew heavier and heavier. At least the mortgage was covered with the insurance. I was getting letters every day in the mail, demanding money. The letters turned into phone calls at all hours of the day and night. I was trapped, alone, isolated and wanted to give up. I desperately needed help. The mortgage insurance soon ran out. My sickness benefit I received did not cover even half my costs, and the debt grew to over $30,000. I was being taken to court, and the house was going to be sold under me. I had no choice but to sell.

It felt like I was giving up. I had no more options. I was beaten, bruised, and terrified. I had invested my mother's inheritance, my heart and soul, hours and years of hard work. I had sacrificed, fought and fought. I wanted security, a solid future for my children by holding on. I had neglected Sheila. Myself.

This big empty house was part of the New Zealand dream, but now there were no more little feet running around. The dream my parents tried to create had turned into my New Zealand nightmare. Sheila was lost. I didn't even know who she was anymore. I was all alone, the most isolated I had been for twelve years. My children were gone, my job was gone, my health was hanging on by a thread, and my sanity was slipping away.

I lay in my deep dark pit, my eyes opening and closing, fading in and out of this drug-induced sleep. I would wake up with a fright, shaking, panting, sweating and feeling scared out of my mind. All I remembered seeing were huge hands gripping my neck. The smell of his filthy bourbon breath in my face was terrifying, his heavy weight bearing on my chest, and insults being screamed in my ears.

'Bitch, slut, whore, useless, fat, ugly, you will never make it on your own!'

Those words echoed through my mind before I woke up in fright. I'd close my eyes and it would start all over again. This continued relentlessly, drowning me. I was so exhausted and tired, but this thing would not let me sleep. I missed my parents and wished I could talk to them. I recalled a rare moment of affection my mother showed when I had been very sick as a child with whooping cough. She was sitting up at night with me, mopping my brow with a cold cloth, singing to me. She sang a song called, 'You Are My Sunshine.'

I tried to picture her here with me now singing those words, 'You are my sunshine, my only sunshine, you make me happy when skies are grey, you never know dear how much I love you, please don't take my sunshine away.' I sang this over and over, trying to drown out the darkness that consumed me. The doctor had a name for it, chronic post-traumatic stress disorder, CPTSD. The pain was unbearable. My leg had become super hard like a piece of granite. It was the clots expanding out of my veins. Any weight on this leg was excruciating. I was in tears by the time I reached the toilet from my bed. My fibromyalgia condition was constantly flaring up every day, giving me more pain and symptoms to drive me crazy. Although I had not always walked the straight and narrow path in life, my belief and faith in God gave me hope. God had delivered me from evil and protected me countless times before. There was no reason to believe He would not come to my rescue once again.

My Beating Heart

Barnz Crawford

I never knew a heart could beat so loudly
But I soon found out—aged 17
A Māori girl walks past me
Red corduroy suit—a mini skirt and black high heeled shoes
Her long black hair—moving in time with her walk
A chill goes down my spine
My heart? What's happening to me? I can hardly breathe

I have only felt this way once before and that was when I was a lot younger, grooming my horse, Dolly. God, I loved that horse!

But then—there she was—"look at me!" my heart was shouting at her. She did—and that was the end of me and my wild ways—sort of

She worked at The Bank of New South Wales in Lambton Quay in Wellington

It is 1967 and on a Friday after work I would wait for her outside the door

It wasn't really a proper door, she had to bend down when she came out

And I would imagine her tripping and falling into my arms

We would catch a bus to my flat at 52 Gordon Street in Newtown and plan our weekend

It's 2022 now and we married on 9 February 1968, 54 years ago

As we were growing up together, I would hear these sayings

"The way to a man's heart is through his stomach," but she hardly cooks because I love cooking, so that doesn't apply to us

She would always tell me the way to her heart is to be kind and respectful to her That's how she treated me—most of the time—and I learnt from that

She asked me once: "Dar, if you die before me, will you wait for me at those Pearly Gates?"

My answer: "Yes, my Darling I will come to get you just in case *y*ou lose your way"

I know that will be hard because I will be happy to see my mum, brothers and sisters but yes, I will wait for you—just like I did on those Friday nights outside the bank in Wellington

You and I have had 3 children—Caroline Vanessa Crawford, Vicky Julia Ray Tommy Pani Crawford, and Haami Gan Crawford we adopted, from brother Waakana and Doe Crawford. You will always be my guardian angel, my darling Polly Smiler Crawford You are my heart my angel, a sweet beautiful-hearted lady. Love you, my V.P.T

We the Bush People

Beverley Smith

My Whakapapa - a short genealogical account.

Early settlers Benjamin and Martha Smith, arrived from England in 1836. They were hoping to make their fortune in gold, but mining in New Zealand and California proved unsuccessful. But in Australia, they really did strike gold. Returning to New Zealand they became respected innkeepers near Papakura. Their third son Ezra became a Forest Ranger during the early wars with Māori, before marrying Maria Plush and settling in Gisborne. He was an enthusiastic poultry fancier and bee farmer. His son Francis, wife Fanny and family lived a peripatetic life - farming and owning bicycle shops in Wairoa and Gisborne – his son Frank our father, armed with a Marine Certificate ran the launch 'Ruapani' at Lake Waikaremoana for the Government Tourist Department.

Our mother Carmine, was the daughter of John Solomon Harrison of Mauritius and Blanche Henderson of Melbourne. John was successful in an allocation of land at Ngatapa and ran a post office and grocery store.

Carmine, her sisters Bella and Marie all met their husbands while working at Lake House. Carmine to Frank, Bella wed Harry the

HBMC. Driver and Marie to Dawson Mole of Wairoa, Painter and paperhanger.

School Days

On school days, our father would leave home ahead of us to go to the cowshed to milk Ivy, our Jersey cow. There was no power in the cowshed, but there was a separator and chip heater. When we arrived at the shed to wait for the bus, we found three buckets filled with hot water; we stood in these wearing our gumboots until we heard the hum of the engine of the approaching bus, then we stepped out of the buckets with very warm feet into our shoes.

The Hawkes Bay Motor Company (HBMC) Bus driver Noel Beale and his family lived at Aniwaniwa, the first stop was at Lake House and if there were no tourists or hotel staff my brothers and I were the first passengers. The bus ambled down to Kaitawa and onto the village of Tuai, ten miles away that was another world from where most of the men had jobs associated with the Power Station. There was the school, post office, butcher's, general store and a haberdashery. A local farmer provided milk from his small herd, unpasteurised of course and children were sent with a billy to a depot on Western Extension where Gertie, a donkey, trotted down the hill carrying two large churns slung across her back. The milk was ladled into the purchasers' containers. Sometimes children would try and tempt Gertie to leave her post, but she knew her route and stuck to it.

The elevation that separated my friends in Tuai was 1,405 metres to our family at Lake Waikaremoana, quite a climb. Tuai village, The NZ Road Services and HBMC Bus carried passengers and freight through the Ureweras. Scenic yes, terrifying—yes, for first time visitors. Nearer to Wairoa alongside the Waikaretaheke River, where at a lower level, plantings of willows made for a picturesque journey: or maybe not, as in summer the dust rising from the gravel road became stifling. In winter, the mud, slush and potholes kept the Ministry of Works men busy. Noel stopped when he saw the farmers' wives standing by their gate, who would give him their orders for items they needed in Wairoa. Noel would cheerfully shop for a variety of goods for them in his lunch hour.

At the old school, three classrooms accommodated the primers with Miss Farrow, Standards 3-6 with Mr Jensen, the headmaster who was dismissed in a cloud of mystery. There were a small number of High School students. Mr Newick and later Mr Orgias continued our education. Māori pupils attended a separate school Kokako with headmaster Mr Cook. His two daughters attended Tuai. The Tapper girls June, Jocelyn and Jennifer came to school on horseback.

Olive Harvey followed Miss Farrow and she lived at the Presbyterian Mission with Sister Kearney and they became lifelong friends. Olive wrote One Act Plays and verse, such as:

Big boys, little boys, boys as big as I am
Took a gun and went to hunt animals in Siam.

Our spiritual welfare was catered for by Deaconess Sister Janet Kearney. Some of us school children sat the Bible study exams and were fortunate to win a book prize. Every Wednesday afternoon Sister Kearney conducted Girls' Life Brigade for us where we learned to tie knots, took a temperance vow and were read to from Beecher Stowe's "Uncle Tom's Cabin". Did guilt surface in young minds about this tragedy of slavery in another land?

There was a Dental Clinic within the old school grounds. A District Nurse lived in Rotten Row and patients sat on the lawn to wait for her attention.

During my time, we had *one* school outing when we travelled to Wairoa on a hired bus to view a film on T.B. A waste of petrol.

The Country Library service brought us books which we soon read. Friend Colleen tells me we were deprived children. Fortunately, our family had the Arthur Mees Encyclopaedias that were very useful for preparing morning talks, and from which I learned basic French. Our father subscribed to the National Geographic Magazine. Stamp collecting also improved my knowledge of the world. On visits to Auckland, McKenzies and Woolworths sold stamps for collectors. These came in small see-through envelopes and were quite the most exciting purchases.

We committed to memory the wonderful poems of Tennyson's 'The Splendour Falls on Castle Walls' and Wordsworth's 'I wandered Lonely as a Cloud', Belloc's 'Do You Remember an Inn Miranda?' 'Young Lochinvar' by Walter Scott and Walter de la Mare's 'Silver'.

We learned country dancing and the school had a Maypole.

I am grateful to Mr Newick, who just before one Christmas invited us to his home and introduced us to Carols. I thought 'The Holly and the Ivy' was wonderful and Brahms Lullaby so haunting —my first musical experience.

A burst of applause and excited murmurings from children arose as Santa Claus strode into the village hall and joined the headmaster on the stage. The school teachers with the help of local women had arranged a Christmas party for the children. I was allowed to stay the weekend with Gill, her sister Margaret and parents.

I was touched when Mrs Niccol asked what kind of gift would I like? I replied: "A poetry book".

As was the norm, Gill's mother wrote to my mother to ask if I could stay the weekend and this was always permitted. This was reciprocal, as Gill often came up to the lake. Before we visited each other's homes, our mothers would write a short formal note 'Dear Mrs Niccol-Dear Mrs Smith' – no first names, and the kindly Noel Beale never charged my friends for the ten-mile bus trip.

It was during a weekend at Gillian's home that I developed measles and stayed for two weeks in a darkened room, where Mrs Niccol, a nurse before her marriage, looked after me so well.

Back to the Christmas party. The ladies provided reindeer milk—iced milk with vanilla flavouring. We found it deliciously tantalizing, knowing there were no actual reindeer in the antipodes, but the mystery remained. That was until a reunion, decades later, when a mother revealed all.

The hour came when Father Christmas distributed the gifts. I'm told that when his name was called, Barry Brien walked over to receive his gift and said to Father Christmas 'g'day Jim'.

My pleasure knew no bounds when I unwrapped my present to find "The Children's Treasury – A book of Verses for Young Children." I still have it. I particularly liked William Blake's 'Laughing Song'. There was one Tennyson poem, but mostly the verses were admonishments about children's behaviour!

Living in the Wops

In Winter, after a snowstorm, our mother kept us home for a day or two as she feared her three children might become stranded when the HBMC bus didn't make it. Not only for the last five miles but once nearer Wairoa, the Waikaretaheke River rose on the flats and reached the windows of the bus.

After a snowstorm, the following days were often sunny and we children dressed warmly, and wearing gumboots played in the sparkling white wonderland of our 40 acres. Our father bought hay for Ivy, our jersey milking cow, and she dined gratefully, her meal spread on a white tablecloth.

Living at Waikaremoana our bread and meat were delivered twice a week from Wairoa on the HBMC Bus. Our mother tended a splendid vegetable garden, raspberries and gooseberries grew in abundance. In the summer we dug potatoes. And we picked peas and beans. One of my favourite vegetable dishes was onions in white sauce and I recall the evening that I had stomach pains and was put to bed very disappointed that I was missing my special.

In the 1940's cattle and sheep made the long journey on foot through Te Urewera to Rotorua and farmers and locals would put the drover up for the night and give him a meal. Our father treated all our livestock with great care. Sometimes when a bull calf was born, a drover would offer his services for the castration. A docile steer would spend its life roaming around the paddocks before going to the butcher. An electric fence around the bull paddock restrained a more aggressive animal.

The next morning, the drover thanked my parents for his bed and meal (my dinner) and went on his way. It was a Saturday and my stomach was still sore. It was arranged that Dad would drive me to see the District Nurse at Tuai, so off we set in the Bedford truck. The Nurse wasn't sure what my complaint was.

"Maybe appendicitis, Mr Smith," she said. "I suggest you take Beverley to Wairoa Hospital."

Thirty-five winding miles and one hour later I was in a bed at Wairoa Hospital with Dr Riddell giving me a prod here and there and a bed near the door, just in case. It was the longest week of my life and being without books was just awful. But life improved when the lady in the bed next to me, Mrs Delatour, gave me some magazines. And Mr Niccol, Gill's Dad brought letters from my school friends.

The stomach pain ceased and Dr Riddell suggested it may have been a 'grumbling' appendix and made arrangements for my discharge. I dressed and a nurse kindly lent me her comb, which wasn't very clean, but I put it through my hair and went home with my Dad in the Bedford.

I didn't go home alone. Nits, kutu, in French *poux de tete*—it didn't get better. Head lice infected the entire family. I suffered such embarrassment when my mother instructed me to ask for a fine-toothed comb at the general store in Tuai and with infinite patience and with vinegar, she combed through every strand on every head and within a week the Smith family were clean.

The Lindy Fiasco

Our nearest neighbour was a retired roadman, William John Lindegar, Australian-born, a private in the Otago Regiment and was a survivor of the Battle of the Somme He is now buried in Wairoa, Hawke's Bay cemetery along with fellow R.S.A. soldiers.

Our father called on Mr Lindy twice a day. One morning: "Bill, I'll take your order for the butcher," father said: "Bev will pick it up after school tomorrow. What would you like?"

"I fancy a piece of corned beef for the weekend", replied Bill passing over a ten-shilling note. "And tell Bev to buy herself an ice-cream".

One of life's tortuous and humiliating events which is forever attached to my memory is the Friday evening I had, as instructed, bought a very fine piece of corned beef for our elderly bushman. Unfortunately, I left the parcel on the public seat at the bus stop and next morning I was sent in a somewhat emotional condition on the HBMC bus to retrieve it. This bus connected with the Road Services bus enroute to Rotorua. On the return trip with the soggy parcel (no plastic bags in those days) on my lap, sitting left front of the bus and opposite a good-looking young man, absolute, intensified mortification set in. I realized my parcel was leaking and a watery bloody substance dribbled down my lap and leg.

When I reached home my mother took the offending package, unwrapped it, rinsed the maggots off and then sent me up with it to Mr Lindy's. I can report that he lived to a ripe old age. There was usually a reward from Mr Lindy – an invitation to partake of as many chocolate biscuits as one could eat, from a large square tin. He was also generous with half-crowns that I put in my English pillar box red tin money box, then with a knife tried to slide them out!

Mr Lindy lived in a roadman's hut, amidst a gooseberry patch where a gentle stream flowed quietly at the end of his garden. Mr Lindy's hut - courtesy of the Ministry of Works who in the bygone days provided accommodation for their roadmen who worked in isolated areas. In the 1950's although retired, he was the recipient of a fine new hut.

Mr Lindy was a great reader; he had a local paper delivered; Noel expertly flicked it over the bushes. He would pass on his reading matter to us and we enjoyed: *The Australian Journal* and *Walkabout,* but we children were not permitted to read *Truth.* Of course, when lighting the wood range in our kitchen or wrapping up scraps in newsprint we did read the salacious articles of the time.

After suffering an injury on a farm, when a horse he was riding fell on him, leaving him with a severe limp and using a stick, he worked as a roadman for the Ministry of Works. With our father, they would select fallen logs and put them on a 'flying fox' to transport them down to a clearing near his hut. Mr Lindy then cut the logs up with a four foot lightning hand saw to fit his fireplace. Mother filled two half tanks with stove size wood and we children armed with a tomahawk would chop to kindling size.

Each Christmas Day our mother would send me up with a hot roast dinner for him.

Grey Rain

One morning in 1954 we found that all our paddocks looked grey in colour and on investigating our father discovered that the grass was covered in a fine ash.

Our father was the hotel projectionist, one of the many varied tasks he took on. The films were distributed by the National Film Unit to the Government Tourist Hotels and we were supplied with a diet of black and white Wallace Beery and Margaret O'Brien pictures, quite wholesome fare, always preceded by a magnificent tourist attraction such as '*Walking the Milford Track*'. The audience - a few tourists and staff of the Hotel.

"I can smell sulphur," commented our mother on the way home. She was no stranger to the aroma, having worked at a hotel in Rotorua, but more recently had placed a saucer of it in a sick room. The boys had suffered whooping cough and a common antidote for fumigation was to place a sauce of burning sulphur in the sick room. On entering the kitchen, Mother looked at the boys. "What have you got in your hair and your clothes smell?" She reached into a cupboard, took out a saucer and placed it outside. A few minutes later she brought it back inside and found it full of ash.

"There's been an eruption, a volcano has erupted," our father explained. "Probably Mt. Ngauruhoe, I heard on the wireless that it was active."

Our clothes were put in the washhouse and we cleaned our faces and wiped our hair before going to bed.

Next morning, we children were quiet, as always when our parents listened to the news and indeed, we heard that Mt Ngauruhoe had erupted, but no one had ever considered that the force of nature would affect a farm so far away.

Our father went out to the porch where the telephone was attached to a wall and rang the hotel; the Receptionist rang the Wairoa Exchange and eventually he was connected to a farmer—Mr Begg.

"Allan, Frank Smith here, could I come down and buy some hay. The farm is covered in ash and the animals need some fodder. Rain is forecast, so everything will be washed clean. Goodness knows what the milk will taste like if they drink from the streams."

Indeed, heavy rain did follow and for a few days, we children pulled faces as we had no choice but to drink either milk or water.

Mother collected more ash and put it into a small glass container. It now resides in my china cabinet.

Our Pets

"Beverley, you mustn't bring your kitten to school." I looked up to hear the headmaster addressing me. I didn't offer the explanation. The previous day, a girl in our class who lived at Wilson's Mill, asked me if I'd like a tabby kitten, so that evening I asked my parents who agreed to having a new family member, as it was not so long since Tinker, the big black cat, had gone to Cat Heaven.

Wilson's Mill is about a half mile off the main road between Tuai and Kaitawa and Mr Andy Nugent ran a school transport service for the six children, using his covered-in truck that had seats around the side. It was not the most satisfactory way of conveying precious cargo. That was part one of the journey for the little kitten.

At 4 pm. I boarded the Hawkes Bay Motor Company bus to take me and kitten to Waikaremoana. I'm not sure if Noel Beale, the driver, noticed. If he did, he was so good-natured not to comment.

Enid Blyton provided a name for our kitten – he became Chinky. Although he appeared to be a healthy youngster, it was sad that his time with us was not very long. He became sick and died, probably 'put down' as the expression goes!

Tinker was my favourite cat. I can still feel Tinker laying on my chest, with his head tucked up under my chin, contentment for human and cat.

Every summer some merciless Wairoa folk would liberate an unwanted Christmas present: the gift of a kitten was very exciting, until it became a bother that no one wanted to care for. That was the situation of the arrival on our doorstep of a very pregnant black and white cat that waddled down the grass track to our home. Our mother let her give birth to her kittens in the warmth of the hot water cylinder cupboard. I can't remember how many she had, but we were allowed to keep Roger the Lodger, who grew into a beautiful cat and provided many happy memories for our family.

I must mention Patches – a black calf I was fond of and I think she was fond of me, but perhaps only for the fresh grass I picked and proffered her on the other side of the fence. Patches wasn't a milking cow and I was very affected when our father sold her to the local butcher.

One more memory: One day after a drover and his flock had meandered past the top gate, a beautiful white kid was left behind and our father brought him home. The baby goat was the most adorable pet: sweet smelling, so clean and didn't mind being dressed up and placed in a doll's pram. It did have one habit that we had to watch: sometimes the oven door was left open and it would hop in: We always rescued it.

On occasions when I had a friend to stay, we were permitted to join a Lake House Hotel launch trip on the Tourist Corporation launch 'Ruapani' skippered by our father. One afternoon, on the return journey, sitting at the back of the launch, two young women, obviously city types, launched into song. That day Colleen and I learned the tune and lyrics of 'Ten Green Bottles'. The visitors imbibed the beauty and history of the area and two country girls' knowledge of life outside Te Urewera was enhanced.

At Lake House, the hotel staff went occasionally to the Saturday night pictures being shown in the Tuai Hall driven by Noel without any admonishment from his employer. I was considered too young, but got to know about the 'sing song' that took place on the way home. In the heart of the Ureweras, when the bus headlights would pick up a wayward rabbit or hare that ran and ran as they sang 'Run Rabbit Run,' or a family of snuffling pigs with Noel coming to a halt to let them pass. 'Don't Fence me in', or a parody called 'Rosie Bay, Rosie Bay, you can see Panekerikiri far far away' sang the housemaids, the waitresses and the laundry maid on board.

Although life was simple and we didn't have so-called city advantages, no music lessons. We did have a cosy home, good food and a fantastic landscape to explore.

Haiku

Beverley Smith

Submerged memories
Rise to the surface like fish
After dragonflies

Petrified forest
Gravestone of another age
Memento of time

Hibiscus flowers
Uniform in red and green
Command attention

Random thoughts and woes
Are like undisciplined weeds
Growing in our souls

Shearing Life

Molly Pardoe

I'd like to think that summer is such a fun time of the year
Except when you're in a shearing gang, there were lots of things to fear
No modern comforts in those good old days, piled into the Bedford truck
Just settle in and hope that you'd be blessed with real good luck
As we squashed up together with all the gear piled high
The long – dusty – windy roads, all we could do was sigh
Working from five in the morning, with little time to rest
You had to keep going at 100 miles an hour, to keep up with the best
As a really new kid on the block, I found this hard-working crew
Far too focussed on their tasks, to realise that I was so new
The heat was really indescribable, those tin sheds were like a sauna
Just had to keep on going and hang out for the break and a cuppa
Why did I say yes and join this hard-working mob
I used to be a secretary, it was such an easy job
I was trying to impress my boyfriend of the time, with feelings quite intense
Was I completely insane and out of my mind, to let my heart rule

common sense?
I thought the work would be easy, just sweeping with a broom
But there was wool flying everywhere, definitely not much room
To sweep at every moment as the fleeces continued to fall
This community of shearing folk, is definitely not much of a ball
But the shock really got to me with the start time at 5 a.m in the morning
To work all day long to 5 pm I wasn't given any warning
How tough this endless stint would be and the expectations of the crew
Never mind my aching hands and body, sympathy from very few
It was early in the 1960's and everyone was super keen
To go hard and make their fortune, but the work was never a dream
The sound of sheep and lambs, nonstop Baaaa!
The smell of their poo and pee, yuck, why am I here – NAH
It wasn't modern living, the quarters were pretty bad
It was common to be sleeping communally, was I really that mad
Some of the folks I hardly knew, but we had to tolerate each other
And that's the way it was then, suck it up, or go home to mother
Shearing was the name of the game, definitely not for the meek
Think of the dollars we'd get paid at the end of the week
I'm longing to go home and enjoy the rest of the summer
Damn half of it is already gone. Oh, what a bummer!

Summer is Almost Gone

Molly Pardoe

Summer is almost gone, as I sit and take time out
It's been over two years since Covid tossed the world about
I'm watching the clear blue sky now, vivid as can be
As the leaves in the trees dance to and fro, dancing, oh so free
The garden is full of colour; red, white, pink n blue
Providing us with this brilliant picture, which is free to view
Isn't nature wonderful, if we just understand
That we need to work together, always hand in hand
To take care of our planet, allow our children to be free
From pollution of every kind, in the sky, on the land and sea
As the seasons change, we understand how ruthless man has been
Just destroying everything in his path, forgetting the current scene
Floods, fires, famine and heartache, people escaping for their lives
Men fleeing from their country, often estranged from children
and wives
What can we do to change the world and keep respect in tact
Understand, that profit before people doesn't work, that's a fact
We see it in our country now, the imbalance of rich and poor
The homeless and the social issues are right on our front door
Like a family who needs to belong and care for each other

Nature is the same, to survive, we need each sister and brother
To carry on the future, from now and remain staunch and strong
And truly believe that together, nature and mankind can belong
Share this planet with everyone, sing the praises of creation
Then we can live in harmony, with the world and this our nation

Climate Change IS Real, Live and Love Our Planet!

Waves at Bliss

Arieal Sage

I see her blonde hair whistle in the wind,
Eyes slowly drop to golden crushed shells.
She's fighting waves, so strong she suffocates.
Thrown back and forth by the currents of her thoughts,
She sinks to the perished pit where she becomes nothing but bits.

Toes dug into its crust, she emerges, a new soul.
An unrecognisable figure stands before her reflected in the glass.
The sand scrapes at her skin, just like her nails do to her flaws.

Looking into her eyes, a story unfolds beneath the icy lens.
They drift to the sky to find peace in mind.
Eyes replicate the ocean's actions. Her smile, as grey as the sky above.
And her heart stone cold, not even the sun could reverse that solid mould.

That morning, when the sun rose and kissed her flawed face.
The silence, ever so comforting, she felt at bliss.
She saw her blonde hair whistling in the wind.
Eyes turned toward the horizon, she finally felt at bliss.

Solo

A *Lucid* story by Christopher McMaster

Solo is written as a reader magnet, or bonus reading material, as part of the *Lucid* trilogy *(American Dreamer, Tomorrow's History,* and *Gods and Dreamers),* published by Dreaming Big Publications, a publishing house based in the United States. With *Solo*, Christopher hopes to introduce readers to the *Lucid* universe (or *universes*) and whet their appetites for the three novels making up the trilogy.

Who will catch the killer, when the killer is from a different reality? It takes a dreamer to stop a dreamer ...

I found him sitting on a stool in the corner of a run-down bar. Real ambiance for the alcoholic, but he wasn't one of those. He was just pretending, like he did with the rest of his life, at least the waking part. I didn't give a shit what he did here, whether he was a drunk, a garbageman, a bagger at a grocery store, or that asshole at the DMV you had to deal with when you renewed your license.

He was the last one, by the way. He actually worked at the Department of Motor fucking Vehicles. But that wasn't why I was going to kill him.

He couldn't see me from where I was standing. I'd wait to introduce myself. Pretending to be a drunk sitting at a bar meant he had to drink, so I'd wait until he had at least two, maybe starting his third. If need be, like if he nursed those two too slowly, I'd buy him that third. He'd take it as well, because he was that type of guy. This was the first real look I'd had of him. Most of what I caught were just glances, or following him from a distance, so far back that he'd never suspect someone was tailing him. I knew the back of his head, the shape of his body, how he walked.

I saw more of what he left behind, after he had finished and was no longer around. That was, literally, the stuff of nightmares.

The bartender looked at me, trying to decide what he was seeing. I gave him a warm smile to sow a little confusion and buy some time. He turned back to his bar and poured a drink for a real alcoholic sitting farther up. I had to be careful with my costume. Even this place didn't want whores inside hassling their Johns, and it was the girls on the corner I modelled myself on. A few changes should be enough to pull it off. Tight jeans with a glittery belt around my waist instead of very short shorts or a mini skirt. A blouse tight enough to show off my tits without revealing too much of them through a thread bare halter top, or a piece of coloured elastic they called a 'tube top' in this time and place. And flat soled shoes rather than heels. I could have probably worn all that other shit and made it work by avoiding the heels, and especially knee-high boots, but why risk it?

It seemed to have worked as the bartender ignored me after he poured the booze hound his drink and went back to whatever he did when pretending to work. He could polish glasses with a rag for all I cared, just as long as he paid me no mind and let me gaze uninterrupted at Mr Wonderful perched on his barstool. His moustache and wide collared shirt gave away the decade. The cheap wood panelling and neon of the establishment was another obvious clue. Only the seventies could produce such tacky décor, and that was in multiple realities. This one had its advantages. A woman in sexy jeans could stare across a low-lit tacky bar at a guy on a bar stool and not be thrown out. Or worse. Here she could even sit next to the guy, buy him a drink, seduce him into leaving with her. That was the plan, anyway.

Sure, he'd first think I was a hooker and guard his wallet, but that third drink would loosen him up enough to see what was on offer was willing and free. He'd even start to believe the lies I told him about his looks or his wit. Stroke his ego, massage it a little, give it a caress. It's not that he's stupid—he might not be, and I seriously doubt he is. And it's not that he's just a man and men usually fall for that kind of shit. It's that he thinks he's safe. That he's home. That nobody knows, or even suspects, what he really is or what he has done, because, quite simply, nobody does. Nobody can. And I look nothing like his type, his usual target. He likes them young and scared, in modest dresses. Not tight sexy jeans.

The thing is, he doesn't even know what he is, because he tells himself it isn't real. But what makes me touch the blade in my hand bag is that I don't believe it. I know he knows that's just a lie he tells himself. And that makes the next part easier.

I walked to the bar, sat on a stool, and waited. It was all about timing. You could only stand around so long until it became suspicious. I lifted a finger without looking at the bar tender. He showed up a moment later and I ordered a bourbon on the rocks. I wasn't there to drink, but that didn't mean I couldn't. I was at a bar. It was a prerequisite for attendance. He set the glass in front of me and I listened for the ice to crack, smiled as it popped, lifted the drink and took a sip. One of life's little pleasures, awake or asleep. I slowly set the glass down and closed my eyes. I turned my face towards the end of the bar and opened them. He was looking right at me. I smiled, pretending to be shy, and looked down at my drink.

I like bourbon. I like the smell, I like the sound of the ice, I like the taste. There's no need to be an ascetic in this work. I'll take another sip, wait, take another, then shoot a furtive glance back down the bar and find him looking right back at me. He may be a monster, but he's also a man. Just like a trout in a mountain stream, with the fly dropping in the water, once, twice, three times, cast and lift, cast and lift ... well, he would take the bait and get hooked. Next cast would be difficult. I could show no revulsion or hatred, no recognition, merely a coy glance and nothing more. He would sense anything else.

There is a street in another reality. Not really a street, more a narrow lane paved in cobbles, lined with terraced houses. They are so close that you can almost touch the buildings on the other side of the lane with outstretched arms. Almost. It is barely wide enough for a horse and cart. The second floor of these houses jut out and cover a couple feet of the lane. At night it is like walking down a damp, dark cave. Not many walk about at night. Especially the young women. That's how I learned about him, though at that time I didn't know who it was. I just felt the fear in the people, especially the young women. They didn't even want to talk about it, but in the end they did.

There was a beast lurking in the shadows. That's what they called him in whispered voices. *The Beast*. So most stayed in at night, while the monster hunted outside. Sometimes, however, it can't be avoided. You have to get home after work. You spent too long with your lover and didn't notice the sun setting and night fall. You have to deliver a meal to your sick grandmother. You refuse to be frightened of the dark and the monsters that lurk in the shadows. Whatever the reason or rationale, you make that fatal mistake.

The result is the same, for the unlucky. He hides in a doorway as she passes, and then jumps on her. He wraps his hands around her neck and squeezes so tightly no air or sound can escape. Her eyes bulge and her face reddens. She tries to resist, but he is behind her and his grip is strong. She is too frightened to think. She flails her hands, trying to rid her back of this predator. She tries to pry loose the hands around her throat. But by this time, she is too weakened by fear and asphyxia. Her vision darkens. Her legs grow weak. Her consciousness flickers and goes out.

When he feels her go limp, he adjusts his grip and lifts her in his arms, carrying her down to a narrower alley, takes her further into the gloom and like a bridegroom carrying his bride, he lays her gently on the ground. Then the bridegroom analogy becomes literal. He doesn't like them awake. For the sense of power, he places his hands back around her neck as he finishes, and to make sure she doesn't join him, that her eyes do not flicker open and meet his. Maybe that is his nightmare—being seen.

My nightmare is what he leaves behind. Below her waist, she is untouched in any other way. He wants everybody to know what a man he is. He positions her legs wide apart, knees bent. There is no mistaking what took place. Above her waist is different. He has carefully sliced along her throat, from ear to ear. Beside his work, placed with care, he always leaves his knife, cleaned from a cut piece of his victim's clothing.

I don't know why he does that. In a future reality those investigating serial killers will refer to it as a 'calling card'. A signature of sorts. Drawing a symbol, leaving a memento, even the way they cut. In one reality another killer's signature was how he mutilated his victims. They called that beast 'Jack'. After five gruesome murders, he apparently vanished. They had no idea how many others may have been cut by that madman in other times or places. There were many. But for them, it was enough to believe he was gone, whoever, or whatever, he was. I could tell them what happened to Jack, if I wanted to, and if I thought they wanted to know. I could even describe the look in his eyes when he realised that he was bleeding profusely from a sharp knife cut made by the blade in my hand.

But they don't want to know his fate. It's enough for them to know he is gone.

Calling cards. Signatures. Splayed legs, a slit throat, and a cleaned knife. Sometimes calling cards led to capturing the monster. Most of the time it didn't, and never would, because the killers have simply disappeared. Those that kill in their own realities can write their cryptic notes or leave their souvenirs. That type of psychopath, the one that kills while awake, scares the hell out me, if I'm honest. Thankfully, there's enough chasing them already, constables or cops, police or detectives, in those realities. Now, those that just disappear … that's what this particular beast does. He finds a quiet and dark place, slows his breathing and his heart, and wakes up. Somebody has to track *them* down, and it sure isn't going to be Sherlock Holmes. He wouldn't know what to do with the clues of this case.

I lift my glass, breathe in the rich earthy scent of the bourbon, lift it to my mouth, and sip. It flows across my tongue and I let it linger before swallowing. I lick my lips, furtively glance down the bar and briefly make eye contact. He is not used to women looking back, but he is off guard, because he doesn't know how dark this particular alley is. In another few minutes I'll get up and sit next to him, maybe leave a barstool between us. He'll see my glass is almost empty and offer to buy me another. If he doesn't do that, I'll help him and tell him to. I watch as he takes another drink from his glass. His second is almost empty. It is time.

"God has left us," one girl whispers.

"Do not blaspheme," her companion hisses.

They are terrified and traumatised. This is a result he never pays attention to, though he preys on it.

"He is a devil," the first continues. "He just walked into the shadows as if they are a door back into hell."

The shadows are a door, but not into hell.

I waited until the corpse of his latest victim was removed, after the place was blessed or protected by the priest, after everybody had left. I lit my candle and examined the scene. A large stain of blood marked where she died. I scanned an arc of cobbles leading away from the spot, holding my candle close to the ground. I moved from right to left, slowly, attentively, one yard away, then two. And then I saw the first of his prints, an inky spot on the cobbles. Almost another yard forward was another, and another. He stood in her blood, and carried it where he went. The prints led me to a dark corner, where they stopped, two bloody footprints. I used the candle to search forward, to look for more prints, but there are no more. They seem to simply disappear into an invisible door.

I looked at the buildings around me and saw a soft light. A curtain moved. I was being watched. I went to the house the light belonged to and knocked. There was no answer, but I knew somebody was inside. I knocked again, but softly.

"Is anybody there?" I asked, three simple words telling them I am female, I am harmless, I am like you.

"Please," I added.

I heard movement behind the door, whispered voices, a quiet argument. Finally, the door cracked open, they see me, and the door opened wider, swallowing me whole. I stood in their home, relieved and humbled. They were terrified, and yet they still give shelter and succour.

"You must not be out at this time!" I am chastised.

"Thank you," I said meekly, and they led me to a small hearth where a fire burned dimly. They sat me down as if I were made of explosives. I told them I lost my way, that I saw the stains on the stones, that I grew frightened. Finally, they decided to trust me and speak.

"God has left us," one girl whispered.

"Do not blaspheme," her companion hissed.

"He is a devil," the first continued. "He just walked into the shadows as if they are a door back into hell."

Her face drained of blood as she told what she saw. A man, or a devil in the form of man. Covered in blood, his hands and arms stained red, walking nonchalantly up the ally, stopping beside a wall, standing there for a moment, and then simply fading into nothingness.

"What do you mean, fading into nothingness?" I asked.

"He ... it ... I could see a man, even in the dark, and it ... his body became lighter—"

"Lighter?"

"I was able to see through it. Not at first, but more and more, until it looked as mist or fog. Then he was gone. Completely gone!" She started to sob and was comforted by the other.

It is the confirmation I sought. I do not press them farther than they can bear. I take a cup of warm soup from them, thank them, and accept their offer of shelter for the night. When they wake in the morning I will be long gone. When I am certain they are asleep I creep out of their home and stand in the alley where the blood stains end. I empty my mind of thoughts, except for one, an intention, a focus, on the man who made those bloody marks on the stones and where he opened his eyes. Where he woke up.

I closed my eyes and thought of that place. I saw the black curtain in my mind that was left once the light was removed, and I stepped behind it. If there was a witness watching, they would have seen my body become lighter, until it looked as mist or fog, and then completely disappear. When the dark begins to clear, I see more shadows, until my eyes adjust to the gloom of an alley across from a tacky bar, where nobody notices a woman mysteriously appearing out of thin air.

I am tempted to order another drink. I really need it. I am tempted to wake up, to close my eyes and open them to familiar light. Not shadows or dark curtains, and what lurks in and behind them. This is a godless place.

But that is why I am here. There are no gods. Or they simply do not care.

Psychologists say dreams are the psyche's way to communicate with itself. They are a way for the subconscious mind to tell the conscious mind what it does not know and what it does not understand. Dreams are spontaneous manifestations of the unconscious. Dreams do not deceive; they do not lie. They are as simple or as complicated as the dreamer themselves. Dreams are individual. We need to understand what they are expressing through their imagery and symbols in order to understand ourselves, et cetera, et cetera.

Some of that might be true. We all dream, even if we don't remember every single one. And dreams serve a purpose. Sometimes. They can help cleanse our subconscious or inner mind. Like parasites burrowing to the surface of our skin, inner traumas or confusions or worries, through dreams, they surface and we let them go. Maybe, at times. I'll give them that much. But sticking to that kind of thinking is just a form of masturbation. Self-obsessing, self-analysing, narcissistic ... to think that it was all about you and your problems or fears or neurosis! That's just wanking.

I think of dreams more as a multi-layered, multiversal energy that contains us all. And existence is energy, and like life, wants to continue. This energy feeds off other forms of energy, just like all life on earth feeds on other forms of life. We consume the living to continue living. Everything on the planet, even trees sucking up the nutrients of past life from the soil where they root. What people refer to as 'gods' do the same, only the energy that nurtures them comes through belief. To continue to exist, they need us to worship or fear or honour. They need our energy. They use us to shape realities, to push events in certain ways, so they can continue to feed on worship or fear or honour.

And I learned I wasn't the only person awake in my dreams. It is not too hard to wake up in a dream, to be aware that you are the dreamer, and realizing that what is around you in the dream is real, at least for those that call it their reality. Try it. Go to sleep with the intention of waking up in your dream. Usually, the awareness that they are conscious in a dream is enough to make most wake up, but with practice, it is possible to stay and experience a time and place that seems dream to you, yet is very real to those around you. Imagine it—whatever is done greatly impacts those inhabiting that reality. Controlling lucidity and moving through our multiverse is very powerful.

The energies we call gods use this power. They use dreamers to push realities in directions that create cultures that perpetuate their myths, even if that is based on fear. Scared people search for security, safety, protection, and deities provide just that, at least in story. It is enough for both human and god. Most helping the gods don't even remember what they have done. There are many that do, that live for sleep, that live to dream, so that they can please their god. Ancient peoples knew this. Their stories and sagas are filled with tales of gods interfering, meddling in the affairs of man, but they need hands to do so, and their devotees willingly offer theirs.

In realities that have no knowledge of Mariam of Okhum, then a devotee helped push your world in a direction towards patriarchy and war. She is unknown in those places because she was suffocated in her crib by the hands of a dreamer. In other realities a young president was shot, with the gunman captured insisting he was a patsy—because he was. The real person firing the fatal shot was never caught, because she was no longer in that reality. She woke up. In others a Macedon named Alexander became The Great, and ruled an empire that covered the known globe until he died an old, old man. Elsewhen, he died a young man, after conquering half a globe, poisoned while on campaign, or he was killed in his crib, or he was not even born when his mother, Olympias, met an untimely end. There are too many examples, from many, many realities.

There are also dreamers trying to stop the devoted ones. That's why the library at Alexandria never burned, how we enjoy Christopher Marlowe's plays, why the western hemisphere is Chinese ... in some realities, anyway. Resisting the gods. Good luck with that, right? Those resistors are mostly just trying to protect what they call reality, which means being there to stop other dreamers.

They both tried to recruit me, but I prefer to work alone. I saw another type of dreamer, one that also works alone, and I think my energies are best spent there. I don't see I have much choice, because I don't see any others trying to stop them. But I don't stop a dreamer; I find them and I wait until they're awake. When they're awake, it is playing for real. That kind of death is not one they'll wake up from. I find them while they are feeling safe in their own reality, where a bartender thinks they're just another drunk, their colleagues think they're just another incompetent bureaucrat, and their mothers think they're a good son.

Sometimes it is a daughter. But not very often.

I climbed on a barstool one away from his and set my empty glass down. My eyes went to him, then shyly back to my glass. As if on cue, an ice cube shifted in the bottom.

I have a ritual of sorts before entering the dream state. I prepare my bed, propping pillows so that I recline more than lie. I turn off the lights and lie down, close my eyes and clear my mind by meditating on my breath. Just watching the air go in my nostrils, and then out, which settles my mind, tells it that its day of thinking is over, and that I need it to focus. Breath in, breath out. I then concentrate on the emptiness of no-thought, on the black behind the black you see when eyes are closed. As I sink deep into this blankness, I hold an intention. Intention is the key. Whether it is simply to remember a dream, or to go to a specific time or place, it is intention that directs the mind. With practice, an intention can be visualised as an image, or an icon, a manifestation of the meaning behind what is intended.

I held an image of my intention fiercely with concentration, the place she was killed, the darkness of night, a later night, when he would kill again. And I sank into the blackness, maintaining a thread of awareness as my body drifted into sleep. I just had to smell the air to hunt him. That scent of fear. Fear was his power. I breathed in the smell of his presence, and opened my eyes. I was in a dark lane, wearing the same skirt and smock as the other women, though no one, woman or man, was out at this time. Almost. I listened to the night and heard a soft noise, a distant breathing. I hoped it wasn't what I thought.

Gathering up the loose fabric of my dress, I crept forward, knowing I was already too late, at least for the young woman under him. His seventh victim. By the time I slipped around the corner, hiding in the shadows, her body lay on the cobblestones, legs splayed and blood flowing from her throat, soaking into the fabric of her bodice and the stones beneath. Ignoring her, I stepped past, and then I saw him. His back was turned as he faced the wall of a house. I knew his eyes were closed, and he was falling into a blackness of sorts, falling awake to his own reality. I watched him begin to grow translucent as he left this time and place, disappearing into the night. But before he vanished completely, I latched onto his image and followed, closing my eyes, falling forward, not onto the blood-stained cobbled lane but into his waking.

When I opened my eyes, I saw a brownstone building, beginning to wake for the new day. Fresh sunlight bathed the street. My only company at this time in the morning were the birds hidden in the trees above. They were the only things singing in this place. I marked the scene firmly in my mind, the look, the feel, the smell. It would be the intention I would use to return to this waking, when I would wait for him to leave the safety of his apartment, his bed, and emerge outside in the reality where he felt safe. I would follow him down the seedy street to his favourite seedy bar, where I could sit next to him and he could buy me a drink.

"I'm empty," I said with a shrug. That I have to wait at all says so much about the guy. Finally, he lifted a finger to the bartender and mumbled something like, "two of those."

"Doubles," I added, smiling. I flash it at my target, a nice shiny lure, followed by a jokey tug at the line. I seem to like fishing analogies today. "Their bourbon is so weak!"

He smirked in reply.

I softened my face, trying for inviting, safe, horny. I could see I pulled it off. He relaxed, as if that inner battle with his rational mind ended and I won. He's not used to this. Women don't approach him, even in a place like here. I caught a glimpse of the frightened little boy lurking deep inside him, but I pushed that image away. I'm not here to save children. I am here for the man who rapes and kills young women.

When the glasses arrived, I indicated to the stool next to his and he nodded. I moved closer.

"I need this after the day I've had," I told him. "Thanks."

"My pleasure," he responded.

I make up a story about a shitty boss, a frustrating job, and he nods. He can relate to that. I tell him that even with the sun shining outside I sometimes want to just hide from this city. It's no Ritz, he admits, but this place is good to sometimes slink away to. I watch as he sips his drink after I do mine. It's his third and he is loosening up, deciding he likes me and flattered that I seem to like him. Women don't talk to him like this and he likes it. What man wouldn't? The chat continues to float along the surface. I slip in a flirt, a subtle innuendo. It takes him a few moments to realise that that is what it is. He smiles. His guard is down. I turn my head to listen to the music from a jukebox in the corner. The music in this decade is spectacularly terrible.

"Shall we dance?" I ask.

He smiles and nods. I take his hand and am pleased it is already open and waiting. We take a few steps away from the bar and I put my arm around him, placing my palm against the small of his back and slowly move it up. I put the other around his waist and place myself so smoothly against him that he thinks he put me there. I want him to feel my breasts against his chest, my warm body next to his. I feel his hands around my back. One tentatively moves lower. After a few more sways to the music, I encourage it to keep traveling, and it cups my ass. I feel a bulge against my thigh.

We sway some more. His hand is still on my ass. The bulge presses against my leg. I nuzzle my face into his neck. He smells my hair. I know his eyes are closed and he has made a decision. He will take me home.

"I'd rather dance someplace more private," I whisper as the next song starts.

I'll decide what I do on the walk over, or maybe as events unfold. Let him go in first, exposing his back? Surprise him when he starts to undress, pants around his ankles? Wait until he is on top of me, totally lost in the moment, totally vulnerable?

Either way, the result will be the same.

Golden Calves on Silver Screens

Roman Seaton

Those unwanted, outdated,
irrelevant ramblings, unfashionable
and so obtuse.

So restricting, constricting,
conscripting to giving, "feeling bad
for the bad things we do".

"Yes we are free without strings!"
So we sing as we braid, twining
velvety chains for our noose.

Prayerbook liturgy blazed "233°C",
feels good; who's to say it's less true?

"We're godless by group-vote",
says the son to the father,
"you're just an idea in our heads".

Thus through screens we so
scream down our children's
daydreams, neo-hedonist's
ordinations.

Their minds full of steam,
tearing curtain' twin seams,
in breaking of substitute breads.

Having robbed us of faith crawling
forward in their place, Golden Calves
as our compensations.

Sunday comes soon to emptied
streets, chapel bells chime a final
time resounding bloodless toll.

Wrought upon the old church's
gates, enough to make weep
cries cinder heap "*Pater, dimitte illis.*"

What once was nave hell renovates,
full pews applaud new urban lords,
pleasure trading your soul.

Worms work neath once hallowed grounds,
TV in place of Crucifix,
Sublime steps to Ridiculous.

Full Circle

Claire Morgan

Our grandmother was in what she called 'Her Second Childhood' when we were in our first.

She and our other grandparents had a significant role in raising us two children. She was known as Plum in our family. She and Grandad travelled to our house in Tunbridge Wells, Kent, in the Southeast of England, all the way from Greater London by train every school holiday and half terms.

To me she held a kind of magic.

The anticipation and excitement began when her letter arrived on the woven coconut fibre doormat through the letterbox, before they came to announce their expected time of arrival.

The small pale blue envelope with blue ink and her dainty copperplate handwriting was instantly recognizable. At the end of the letter her signature: 'Little Plum.'

Not the word, the picture of a plum—it was a tiny, beautifully formed plum, with a curved stem and that indented line that made it exquisitely and unmistakably our 'Little Plum'.

It was so special—I loved it.

Plum even had a signature tune!

We would be in the kitchen with the radio on and she would suddenly say, "Hark! It's my tune. Hush!"

Holding up one finger (or was it a fairy wand?) everyone would freeze to listen while the famous tune,

"The Dance of the Sugar Plum Fairy" chimed delicately, and I would get up and slowly pirouette just like a beautiful little ballet dancer in a musical box, or Cinderella at the ball! Everything was so lovely, and in that moment, I was swept up with my feelings of rapture by the shared imagination.

The space transformed by joy, until, as if midnight struck, she broke the spell, and Plum turned back to the chores and duties in the kitchen.

The worst duty was teaching me my lessons!

Plum was in a different mood and her double chins quivered with disapproval, like the two ugly sisters put together! She reproached me for my daydreaming and for falling behind at school.

She read, aloud, in scathing tones, my schoolteacher's reports:

"Claire could do better if she tried."

Plum set about it with a determination that was grim.

She chivvied me into sitting up straight, she badgered me into concentrating on my work. She was so strict and demanded the completion of the finest detail.

I hated it.

I remember the feel the red and white checkered plastic tablecloth which stuck to my arms as we struggled, daily, to get through my extra lessons:

Sums, until I had them all corrected,

("There is no such word as can't.") Dictation until all my spelling mistakes had been written out ten times:

("If at first you don't succeed, try, try again.") Composition and Dictation until I had copied everything into my best book.

("There, you see what you can do when you try?") I owe my literacy to Plum. Her patience, determination, perseverance, and her love. She had a belief in me. Her joy in living has been transformative —ever since—unfolding, guiding and inspiring.

Now that I am in my own 'Second Childhood' it is as if I have come full circle. I have arrived, with a belief in myself and feel 'at home' here in this beautiful East Cape Community, though it is so far from my childhood home.

I feel a sense of excitement and anticipation—just as if Plum's arrival were imminent and the magic about to begin!

I can almost hear her voice now, my 'Sugar Plum Fairy God/ Grandmother' saying, "There you see what you can do if you try."

Yes Plum, I do, I am finally a willing student, so let's let this magic begin, shall we?

Reflections

A Creative Non-Fiction Essay

Gillian Moon

My family used to visit this place as a holiday destination when I was a child growing up during the 1970s. We would excitedly pile into the family golden coloured Holden Kingswood; my three siblings and I bouncing around in the back with no seatbelts, (and none required!), while Mum and Dad sat up front, windows down, puffing on Matinée and 'du Maurier' cigarettes. Embedded in my visual memory is an image of the flat, yellow packet of Matinée cigarettes, complete with an embossed golden crown, while the only thing I recall about 'du Maurier' is the name and how sophisticated it sounded. It was the 70's and it was the 'norm' of the times.

We would set off bright and early from our home in Onehunga, Auckland and make the long, often tedious and hot journey of car sickness, mantras of "are we there yet?" and the usually gentle voice of Dad yelling "shut up or I will knock your bloody heads together." He never did—it just meant it was time for us kids to pull our heads in and play 'I spy with my little eye' and/or be quiet. We headed away from our big city home to the sunny East Coast; headed to the place I have now called home for the past thirty years with my four daughters and now three grandchildren. A place steeped in family history/herstory. The birthplace of my beautiful, late mother. A place to connect with extended family, to share memories and reflections. A paradoxical place of feeling connected yet unconnected. Isolated yet belonging. Turanganui-a-Kiwa, Gisborne, Tairāwhiti. A place to let journeys unfold. A place to find myself and make sense of the precious commodity we call life.

I moved to Gisborne in 1990, with my then partner and our six-month-old daughter. I was 24 years old. After a two-year stint in Australia, we returned to Auckland. Mum and Dad had taken retirement and moved to Gisborne. The pull to get away from big city life after the birth of our daughter and Mum and Dad's desire to be around their first grandchild was good enough reason to make the move to my childhood holiday destination. With the removal truck loaded and enroute before us, we packed the remaining essentials into our car and made the journey 'home'. I recall stopping in the Waioeka Gorge on that very hot Autumn day to breastfeed and paddle my feet in the river at Manganuku reserve; I felt the spiritual journey of mother, grandmother and great grandmothers herstorys flowing through me.

The Waioeka Gorge holds a special significance to my family; my great grandparents and grandparents were pioneers who created a home and livelihood post W.W.1 – a place to raise a family and return to 'normal' life after the war. Much of my mother's childhood was spent at the homestead, named 'Raysburn' (after my grandfather's younger brother who did not return from the war). There are numerous stories surrounding my family which are documented in local and national history archives, articles and books.

When I first moved to Gisborne, my Aunty Judith Ellmers (nee Trafford and Mum's older sister), a published author, poet and historian, 'employed' me to type up my grandfather's WW1 diaries to preserve the fragile pages of text that were beginning yellow and fade with age. It was an honour and a privilege to type up these memoirs, however, as a then young woman, I didn't fully appreciate or understand the task or the full impact of WW1 or the influence it has had on generations to come.

I am grateful to my cousin Ian Trafford for successfully and beautifully documenting a narrative style account of our grandfather, Alick Trafford's,) WW1 diary, which was published by Penguin Random House in 2020. It was after reading this narrative that I began to see a bigger family picture, a picture which drew me further into the world of my grandmother, Ivy Trafford nee Newman, who she was and the influence her presence has had on my life.

Ever since I was a young child, I have always had a strong sense of fascination and affiliation with Ivy, a closeness that I have never been able to explain. Ivy Emma Newman was born 29/10/1891 and died 06/05/1968 age 76 years. I was just 18 months old when Ivy passed so I have no 'real' physical recollection of ever 'knowing' my maternal grandmother.

I don't know if I was a strange child, I know I was sometimes anxious and unsure of myself, yet I had regular conversations with Ivy or 'Granna' as she was referred to when spoken about. Ivy was my confidant, I told her everything; my worries, my visions, about my 'knowing and sensing' things, about how I believed my 'job' or purpose in life was to bring people together.

Ivy was from a family of farmers on the Gisborne flats and during WW1 she regularly corresponded with a few local soldiers, including my grandfather, Alick Trafford. Upon returning home from war in 1919, Alick continued to woo Ivy (having decided she was the 'one' while he was away), and they wed in secret 28 June 1921. However, later that year they had a simple wedding ceremony at Riverford (the Newman homestead) and then honeymooned away in Auckland.

Upon their return, married life began in earnest in a 'hut' on a block of land that needed clearing to be eventually farmed. Ivy must have been a very strong, and spirited woman to live and thrive under the harsh conditions in the mountainous Waioeka Gorge. Ivy and Alick's first child was unexpectedly and very sadly stillborn. Ivy, understandably slipped into a deep grief and lost interest in the world around her and retired from her life in the Gorge for a time and sought refuge at her parents' homestead to recover. After quite a long period of time, Ivy slowly regained interest in life again and returned to her home in the Gorge, she even agreed to take under her wing a toddler whose mother had sadly passed away; he stayed with Ivy and Alick for about three months until the father was able and ready for him to return home. Alick and Ivy went on to have five children of their own, - life would have been intense in this remote part of the country, especially during the years of the Great Depression. Ivy was clearly a resourceful, and robust woman who was unafraid of 'mucking into hard work.'

Ivy taught herself to drive the first motor car in the area—a Model T, nicknamed 'Tin Lizzie' and with this skill, she was duly employed by the Public Works Department when the road building through the Gorge began. Her role was to transport workers and supplies through to the work site, sometimes in perilous and flooded conditions. Often, travellers through the Gorge would become stranded and the Trafford homestead became well known for its hospitality for shelter and food. I recall my mother telling me there were always extras around their dinner table. The following is from a 'notice' published in The Gisborne Herald after her passing—"It was by no means unusual for up to 15 people to sit down to a meal at the (Trafford) homestead. The name was perpetuated when Trafford's Hill, the best-known climb between Gisborne and Opotiki, got its name. Mrs Trafford (Ivy) became well-known for her charitable disposition and for a ready wit which smoothed over many rough patches of life in the district. She was always a practical help in crises or in times of sickness." (Gisborne Herald, 11/05/1968).

Ivy was clearly a woman of many talents and skills, along with bucket loads of resilience! Yet it also appears that she was also blessed with kindness and compassion which is remarkable for the harsh and often relentless environment which surrounded such early pioneering families. Ivy was penned the 'Mother' of the Waioeka Gorge during her time there, a woman of strength and compassion who could be depended upon—Ivy's garden was her pride and joy which was also perhaps her meditative space, I like to imagine that Ivy's garden brought a sense of peace into her life; colour into an otherwise grey world.

I have a framed, black and white photograph of my baby self-sitting on Ivy's knee; it sits on my bedroom window sill, I have her crafted wooden hand mirror which has "*Ivy Xmas 1919*", inscribed on it, I have her crockery honey pot where I keep my mala beads, I have a small, dainty, hand painted vase – all reminders of this beautiful, strong, kind woman who I never knew yet lives within me and around me.

My mum often said to me, "you remind me of Granna."

I am beyond proud if I possess even a mere ounce of what this beautiful, brave, kind, graceful pioneering woman, Ivy Emma shared during her time on this earth. I am eternally grateful to the wise and wonderful spirit of Ivy who has watched over me with protective arms my whole life – whose presence and guidance I feel as I sit and complete this writing at Manganuku in the Waioeka Gorge. Where I bathe in this river of life, in this place of spirit where I live with humble gratitude.

Ends.

References / Information sourced from:

Born Beneath a Rainbow: Memories of a Country Childhood, Judith Ellmers, New Women's Press, 1983.

Traffords of the Gisborne & Wairoa Districts. NZ 'Now Thus'. Vivienne May McConnell, 1987

The Waioeka Pioneering Saga, Margaret Spencer, Te Rau Press Ltd, Gisborne, 1992.

Into the Unknown, The secret WW1 diary of Kiwi Alick Trafford no 25/469, Ian Trafford, Penguin Random House New Zealand, 2020.

This City

Gillian Moon

This city is going to break my heart

To the man with his head in his hands
sitting on the steps
in the doorway
of a
forgotten building

To the girl
sitting cross-legged
on the railway bridge
over
the shortest river
in Aotearoa

To the woman
looking forward
in her plastic yellow
rain proof poncho
cycling along

the footpath

To the 4 Square worker
sitting on a white plastic chair
at the side of the shop
taking one last mouthful
checking her watch
as she stands up
break over

To the solitary souls
I notice
because
I am
one
too.
This city is going to break our hearts.

Brain fog

Gillian Moon

Hangs like mist on a dark and windless day
like grounded aircraft
there will be
no high flying thoughts today

Washing hangs
lifeless
forlorn,
depressed
and
dripping in
forgetfulness

Patiently
awaiting
winds of change
to blow away
thoughts encased
in cobwebs

awaiting
the injection of new
life,
ideas,
combinations
for new neural
pathways to light up
in total delight
buzzing with life and
opportunities

new waters
to be tried
and tested
pathways to
explore
leading to
excitement
and
total
overwhelm

leading to
tiredness
fatigue
confusion

as the mist
rolls in again
to settle
on the
brain

imagination and planes
are grounded
no high flying thoughts
today.

A Hair's Breadth

Gillian Moon

Amanda finds herself a mere breath away from becoming homeless. Amanda is a RENTER in 2022. Don't complain. Be grateful. Mantras of lock-downs overlap. This housing 'situation' was brewing way before COVID 19 or lock-downs rattled into global consciousness of pandemic proportions. Does this help Amanda's plight in any way? No, of course it doesn't.

It's raining hard, it's cold and the ceiling is crying tears, trickling down walls, leaving stains of despair. The fireplace tries to jolly up the situation, yet it is old, cracking with age and becoming unhinged and past its use- by date.

Amanda is grateful because she is not living in her car or on the street but she still feels miserable, bleak and almost defeated.

Each sound of the hammer hitting the wooden post of the 'for sale' sign reverberates through her soul ... one pounding thud at a time

going
going
gone.

Each sound of the hammer hitting the wooden post of the 'for sale' sign reverberates through her soul ... one pounding thud at a time

Amanda is grateful because she is not living in her car or on the street but she still feels miserable, bleak and almost defeated.

The fireplace tries to jolly up the situation, yet it is old, cracking with age and becoming unhinged and past its use-by date.

It's raining hard, it's cold and the ceiling is crying tears, trickling down walls, leaving stains of despair. Does this help Amanda's plight in any way? No, of course it doesn't.

This housing 'situation' was brewing way before COVID 19 or lock-downs rattled into global consciousness of pandemic proportions.

Mantras of lock-downs overlap. Be grateful. Don't complain.

Amanda is a RENTER in 2022.

Amanda finds herself a hair's breadth away from becoming homeless.

Untamed Spirits

Gillian Moon

I feel them
before I see
sitting
on
the
edge
of dusk
my ancestors
breath
whispers
my name
caresses
my
cheek
my heart
becomes
still
as i wait
for their message
of hope

to raise
me
from
the
depths
of darkness
I wait
and
wait
until
the black-backed gull
quietly
sitting
alongside
me
erupts
in startling
squawks
of full flight
in realisation
the
sun
has
already
set
into
night.

White Morning

Aimee Milne

White Morning

The dahlias are flowering again after a sweaty summer. The intensity is starting to mull, to a palatable warmth. There are bunny tails and crickets, in dry, cracked earth. Cooler nights, better sleeps. The mornings are fresher, and there is something comforting about the damp smell of dew-soaked earth. White dahlias, the size of saucers. Perfectly symmetrical, solid, and proud, like cheerleaders with pom-poms, they stand to attention.

Hooray, hooray, she's here to start her day!

I take the first sip of coffee, my favourite part. Everyone is still sleeping so I savour the peace. I hold the fat edge of a burly mug between my lips, and enjoy the warmth. The coffee is strong, black, and a taut, tingle, travels to the back of my teeth. A constriction of joy in my diaphragm. I breathe deeply, and with each slurpy sip, my brain clears. Sleep-filled eyes lift, and I am focused, like dew-drop dahlias.

I look at my to-do list.

Yellow

He came with a single yellow dahlia in a retro-brown, 70s pot. It was all he had, he had said, after all the love bombing. I still had fragments of that dirty bomb in my eyes, so I couldn't see. His ex-wife was psycho, he had told me. That's why he had nothing. Just that one dahlia. I let him stay and stay became live.

He asked me to marry him after taking acid one night. He announced it to everyone at the party while I was tripping balls in their front garden. It was weird, but exciting, I guess. I wanted to go home. I didn't feel right. He put me in a taxi and said he would just DJ a few more songs. I didn't make a big deal of it. When he finally walked in the door at 7 am he didn't apologize. He said he'd fallen asleep under a tree, not to make a big deal and of it.

He lied a lot.

He hit, and kicked me on a hard, polished floor in a fancy motel.

"Look what you made me do." he said.

When I finally left, he had everything, and I had nothing. The dahlia was flowering when I left, for the last time. I hated that dahlia. I fucking hated yellow dahlias. I grabbed a rough handful of plant and ripped its twisted roots from the pot. I almost put my back out with the effort. I was breathing like a bull about to charge, stomping and huffing and ripping. I flung it around like a matador's cape, until yellow petals lay squashed amongst black earth and rage.

White Wedding

We bought our first house together two years ago, and I've been planting dahlia bulbs from unknown stock. They're my favourite flower, because they stand out. They're strong and hardy, each one is beautifully individual and perfectly put together with a divine ratio. They always grow back, no matter what. With every bulb I placed in fertile ground, I made a wish.

Please, don't be yellow.

My mother hands me a bouquet and I admire the little, delicate dahlias with pink edges, suited to the vintage, boho theme.

I put on my dress, and tuck wildflowers into my hair. Waiting in a garden-full of white dahlias, our garden, that we've grown, is my groom, and I cannot describe the love. I am ready to go home.

Uta

A retelling inspired by the Horouta stories

Charlie Holland

I sat in the moonlight watching Rona's fingers retract from the outer hills of Mangapapa. The morning chill crept in and tickled the end of my nose so I buried myself deeper under the duvet, but my vagal nerves didn't allow me to get too comfortable. I briefly contemplated the idea that I still had time to change my mind, I could choose to stay here, I could ... just stay.

Sliding out from under the duvet, I made my way to the bathroom to get ready. A packed bag and clothes sat patiently outside my door. Dressing and returning to the bedroom, I bent down to kiss my love goodbye. "I wish I could come see you off," a warm sleepy voice mumbled from our bed.

"I know. I wish you could too, but for now I'd rather you stay safe."

Bubu, our little dog scurried into our bedroom from the lounge. "I'm gonna' miss you too, Bubu," I said, scruffing his furry little head. Bubu sniffed my face impatiently, before jumping up and plonking himself into my side of the bed. "He doesn't even care that I'm leaving," I chuckled.

"He's keeping your spot warm."

"I'll face-time you both tonight."

"Love you, babe."

"Love you both, too!" I replied as I closed the door gently.

Swinging my backpack over my shoulders I grabbed a buttered Weetabix on my way through the kitchen. Outside felt warm; it was t-shirt weather, but I shivered nevertheless when I saw the tall shadowy silhouette standing outside my gate with white plumes billowing from her mouth: Kirirangi.

"Ata marie, Āna," greeted Kirirangi. It was too dark for me to see her eyes and the face-mask she now placed on didn't allow for me to read her expression.

"Ata marie," my eyes darted towards her hand. Kirirangi followed my gaze to her vape.

"I know, I know. It's my last one before we go and then I'm quitting for good."

I laughed at her flimsy commitment. My laugh, a little too loud and out-of-place in these early hours. We jumped into her car. Three small wooden boxes lined with polylactic acid were already packed and placed in the back seat, each sealed with wax to ensure they wouldn't get damaged on our journey, or remain safe if anything should go awry.

"Kua reri koe?" asked Kirirangi.

"As I'll ever be," I replied.

Kirirangi pulled into the marina's car park. I grabbed my backpack from the boot while she carefully carried the wooden boxes down to the wharf. The low humming that could be heard from the carpark, reverberated as we neared. The variations of tonality, pitch and metre became more distinct. Standing next to the waka hourua with their heads slightly bowed were Tā Kiwa, Pāpā P and Uncle John doing karakia for our journey.

"... haumi e, hui e, TAIKI E."

Tā Kiwa looked up and smiled upon seeing Kirirangi and I standing nearby. "Mōrena, korua." He made his way over, took the boxes from Kirirangi and placed them on the stand. Karakia proceeded once again to safeguard our taonga. The morning was growing lighter. We knew we didn't have much longer. Cars came and went, dropping off crew members, each with muffled farewells.

It was hard for me to tell who was who, with our face-masks on in the dim light. Once we were all there, we stood near the waka for our final 'church' before departure. One-by-one we set about doing a RAT test and a temperature gauge. Gradually masks were put away as single lines appeared on each of our plastic rods. With our crew testing negative, a new bubble was formed. Finally, we were able to mihi one another, but still felt that mixture of excitement and anxiousness.

Without warning, sprays of gravel and full beam lights assaulted our senses. A low-riding car with a big engine skidded to a halt and sat above us in the car park like a growling predator. The passenger's door swiftly creaked open. "I have arrived!" A female figure scuttled out in front of the headlights and struck a 'Marilyn' pose. Some of the crew members laughed at her antics while others rolled their eyes. My eyes darted to Kirirangi who was standing with Tā Kiwa and her older brother, Pāpā P.

She did make it, my face expressed.

Looks like it. Kirirangi's face replied.

Ah well, she's here now. I responded with a half shrug. Kirirangi watched as Kanawa headed towards the testing table. A soft coconut scent from her freshly shampooed hair wafted, but it was tinged with the stale chemical smell of smokey peat.

With all our personal QR codes loaded, the tablet was handed to the iwi liaison responsible for communicating with any officials on our behalf, should there be any issues. We knew without a doubt that there would be issues. This lockdown had come hard and fast. The new government's leadership came with more mandates and restrictions to combat the latest COVID variant and the 'Bloom', a horticultural fungicide infestation (HFI) that is wiping out our country's commercial crops and domestic gardens. Our people are sick, hungry and desperate for solutions. And, as our Pacific Ocean bound waka departs, it's our Pacific brothers and sisters flocking to these shores as environmental refugees that we feel for. Too many realised too late, they traded submerging lands of home, for the submerging future of their families.

Our crew moved as a collective to board the waka. The sooner we set sail, the less chance of being stopped by the Coast Guard. With international air travel suspended again, the sea is the safest way to go. Our local Coast Guard unofficially supported our plight by granting us a 'blind' window for two-hours in order to save our heritage kumara, rewi and hue from the HFI and the economically-driven seed banks governed by the Ministry for Primary Industries. To some, we were the rebels; but to those we cared about we were an act of hope.

"Here's the manifest," I said as I took a seat next to Kirirangi. We both looked back at the marina. It felt weird seeing an empty jetty.

"I just want to wave goodbye or something," I mewled.

"Then wave," suggested Kirirangi. I felt kind of silly, but I made my way towards the stern of the waka and waved - at no one, and everyone who remained confined to their own four walls. Kanawa sauntered up beside me and slung her arm around my shoulder, vigorously waved and yelled, "So long, suckers." I laughed.

A wind change swept across our faces and before I even had a chance to register, Kanawa lightly skipped over to the raakau and grasped the rope ready for directions from Pāpā P. He barely looked her way, before she started to wind the rope, feeling the tension and reading the tautness in the raa kei. Her actions were smooth and confident. Once the raa kei was set in place, she wound the rope into a tidy coil and stood looking out onto the horizon. Pāpā P came up beside her silently. In sync, the pair lifted their heads towards the northeast in search of telltale patterns in the clouds, wind and birds.

Out through the passage, our waka glided. Maungahaumi in the very distance dissolved into a mesh of dark greens and sandy greys, then eventually swallowed by the glassy blue quilt that rolled upon Tangaroa"s breath: inhale, exhale; inhale, exhale; inhale, exhale. To keep the authorities at bay, we kept radio contact to a minimum and turned off all connections where possible. Being on the water and the waka always felt surreal for the first few days, and often I would be too excited to sleep when I wasn't on watch. By the third day, the waka grew into an extension of myself, not knowing where my feet and hands ended and the ropes and salty wood began.

We sailed well for our first four days to Mercury Bay, ironing out any kinks before heading on to Port of Avatiu. Our last chance to call home before completely leaving the mainland and going out of cell phone range.

"... What's three months?"

"It's three months," I mumbled.

"This was your idea to go."

"I know and I'm glad I'm going. I'm just gonna miss you, that's all," I said with a quiver in my voice.

"Talk to the stars, I'll hear you."

"I will," I smiled and said goodbye. As I went to return my phone, I caught a snippet of someone else's heated discussion.

"... I am ready. I can't make the waka go any faster ... you just make sure everything is ready for me ..."

Some days feel longer than others on the waka. If I had my way, I would extend all sunrises and sunsets by at least an hour. But for me it was all about the nights, the nights felt like another world. A world of magic and mysticism when the skies were clear and the moon bright. However, when they weren't, the nights could be daunting and overwhelming and all I wanted was ... land. I could never tell Tā Kiwa or Pāpā P how dark nights affected me. That just wasn't the wayfinder way.

On that particular night as we continued towards our island home, the sky was slathered in stars, popping candy for my eyes. It was near the end of my watch and I was far too awake to settle. "How ya' going, bud?" Kanawa slid in beside me on the bench.

"Good," I replied. "Are you alright? It sounded heated on the phone."

"Ole' boyfriend's a bloody idiot sometimes." She smiled, shaking her head slowly.

"Are you still with him?"

"Yeah, for the most part. I needed someone to feed the dogs while I'm away," she laughed, "And he's great around my boy. Better than I am at the moment."

"Oh, hey, That can't be right." I said.

"I wanna' be a good Mum, but I keep falling short of the mark." She said looking off into the distance, "Nim'mind, a fresh start when I get back, aye?"

"Yeah," I yawned. "I'm so tired but can't sleep. My mind's so busy."

"You want something to help you sleep?" Kanawa offered.

"Sure," I replied curiously.

Kanawa unzipped a pocket on her cargo shorts and pulled out a vape. I saw it and shook my head, "No, thanks. I don't really vape," I said.

"This is a very special vape," Kanawa said excitedly.

Inhale. Exhale. I sat on the bench and tilted my head back as far as I could until I could no longer see sails or mast poles in my peripheral vision; creating the illusion of floating high above. The gentle rocking of the water simulated a feeling of drifting or gliding on warm air currents. Eyes, now fully dilated.

Long sparkles danced on the sea's silken surface. I lay on my stomach and lowered my fingers into the water, letting them graze. A slow swirling blur of orange appeared below and as it rose, it brightened until a big elusive eye winked at me. Slowly, yet subtly, an orange tentacle rose out of the water and wrapped itself around my grazing hand, working its way up my arm. The wheke pulled me in whilst rising from beneath. Another tentacle etched its way around my neck, embracing me towards hongi. It wasn't a breath we shared, but rather the salt water. The burn of it up my nose, a weight in my lungs - I began to panic. I am now under the water and can see the rays of sunlight streaming down. I start to kick hard, beating the water around me in an effort to rise towards the surface. My face breaks through ... air! Sweet, sweet, air. But I am alone. The waka drifted away. Sitting on the hull is Kanawa, "Come on, Āna," she calls. I swim towards her as she extends her arm. "Come on," she repeats. Her hand reaches for me and her fingers unfurl; five little tentacles.

"Āna. Earth to Āna," Kanawa sniggered. I looked again and Kanawa was sitting beside me in human form, but I had to touch her to make sure. Kanawa's hand felt cold and clammy and her lips were laced with a translucent blue hue, and there was that smell again, that smokey-peaty smell.

"I ... ah. I don't know what's happening," I stammered. Everything seemed disjointed and I felt confused. I turned to Kanawa, "I saw you. But you weren't you," I managed to stutter.

"It's all good, Āna. What you had, my friend, was the best shit this side of the equator."

"Did I fall asleep?"

"No, you just zoned-out for a minute. This vape is an oil vaporizer."

"I don't do drugs, but I know that wasn't weed," I said trying to keep my bobble-head steady.

"This is the shit. This is the oil that the whole world is talking about. It's Bloom oil, baby."

"Bloom!?"

"Yeah. You just inhaled two hundred dollar's worth. You don't just get high, you have visions or prophecies and I'm thinking by the way you're acting, that's exactly what happened to you. Am I right?"

"Bloom? Jesus."

"Yes, my child," laughed Kanawa.

"The Bloom that we're escaping from!"

"Ironic, huh?" She mocked. "Don't worry, it's airtight ... cough, cough! Black spittle settled on her bottom lip. "There's a sea transfer scheduled for tomorrow night, and then it'll all be gone and no one needs to know."

"Is it worth it?"

"Fifteen million says it is."

Kirirangi appeared on deck and started walking towards us from the Ihu of the waka, "You two can go and get some sleep if you like." Both Kanawa and I smiled and nodded and slowly moved from the bench. "Kanawa, you need to see Kiwa first?"

"Yeah, no worries." Kanawa made her way past our sleeping hull to go talk with Tā Kiwa and Pāpā P as the low moon lit up the stage.

Kirirangi grabbed my arm as I went to walk by, "Āna, when you go to bed, stay there. We're expecting some rough weather tonight, so stay in your bunk until I come and get you." Kirirangi looked me straight in the face. "Say that you understand. Āna?"

"Ae, I heard you," I agreed, but felt paranoid. Could she tell I was under the influence? *Rough weather*, I thought to myself and looking questioningly at the perfectly still night. Who was I to argue, my mind was too 'floaty' to question Kirirangi. I climbed down to the sleeping hull and into my bunk. The gentle wind that had just been brushing my hair suddenly grew stronger. This didn't make any sense, a wind this strong does not just appear within seconds without a build-up. The wind continued to grow stronger chopping at the water's surface, so I gripped the side of my bunk. The chop grew stronger, shaking the waka rather than rocking it. Water churned rapidly and thrashed violently against the waka. Then as suddenly as it began, it stopped. There was silence and darkness, once again.

"... Āna?" I was startled awake. Kirirangi was gently shaking my shoulder. "Come up on deck."

"Oh, Okay. Sorry, I must have slept in. What time is it?"

"No, it's not your watch. It's the Coast Guard. They're doing an inspection," Kirirangi informed me.

"What? Why?" I couldn't put the words together and started looking around wildly, until I saw the empty bunk. The bed was perfectly made like it hadn't been slept in and her bag was gone. "Where is she?" I asked.

"Now, Āna. Move!" Commanded Kirirangi. Just before she left, Kirirangi turned swiftly back towards me, "You understand, don't you? It was either her, or our people."

Dressed, but still unsteady, I lifted myself onto the deck to see large flood lights silhouetting three figures that stood to meet the inquiries of the Guard. Megaphone voices grumbled instructions and demands while flashlights twirled about. Three staunch figures remained calm. Pāpā P stepped forward, "Tēnā koutou. Please, come aboard."

Maia the Kaitiaki

Puri Hauiti

Maia lived with his Nanny Rakai in a small village on the East Coast. Nanny Rakai told Maia many stories of his whakapapa and the history of their pa. One day Nanny Rakai took Maia down to the awa.

"My moko, there are two Taniwha who live in this awa."

"They are brothers, drifting up and down within the tidal currents."

Everyone in the pa knows they are there. No one ever bothers the Taniwha because the old people say they were Tapu. Everyone knew one of the Taniwha was scared of the night, and the other was scared of the day."

One day Maia was curious why the Taniwha were scared of night and day, so he asked his Nanny Rakai. "Hey Nan, why are those Taniwha scared? I thought Taniwha were Kaitiaki and were meant to be strong."

"Kaitiaki can be scared, my moko. I am your Kaitiaki, and sometimes the simple things in life scare me."

"Well, nothing scares me, Nan."

As Maia lay in his bed, he wondered why his Nanny Rakai took him down to the awa in the first place. The next day he rushed down to the awa and started calling out to the Taniwha, who was scared of the night.

"Hey, Taniwha of the day, show yourself. Hey Taniwha, hey Taniwha!"

The Taniwha heard Maia's call and arose from the awa in the form of a large Kahawai.

"Kia ora e tama."

"Kia ora Taniwha, why are you afraid of the dark?"

"I am afraid of what I cannot see. I cannot see what's around the corner. I cannot see what's in front of me, and I cannot see what's behind me, hence the reason I only come out during the daytime."

With a whip of its tail, the Taniwha was gone. Maia could now understand why the Taniwha was afraid of the darkness. That night Maia went back down to the awa and called out to the Taniwha of the night.

"Hey, Taniwha of the night, show yourself. Hey Taniwha, hey Taniwha!"

The Taniwha heard Maia's call and arose from the awa in the form of a large Tuna.

"Kia ora e tama."

"Hey, Taniwha, why are you afraid of the daytime?"

The Taniwha looked at Maia and replied, "I am afraid of what I can see. I see a changing world, and it's not the same world that I remember from many years ago. I don't wish to see it anymore." With a whip of its tail, the Taniwha was gone.

Maia could now understand why the Taniwha of the night was scared of the daytime. He headed back home to tell Nanny Rakai about his visit with the Taniwha.

"Nan, I visited the Taniwha and found out why they were scared. I feel sorry for them because they don't get to spend any time with each other. You always tell me that whanau comes first. How can they put each other first if they cannot spend time with each other?"

Nanny Rakai was proud of her moko and gave Maia a greenstone taonga.

"This is a special taonga my Kuia gave me. Wearing this taonga will allow you to find out those answers. It has a special magic that will guide you on your journey. It may also give you strength to bring light into darkness and darkness into light."

He jumped up and hugged his Nanny, saying, "Nan, you are magic," and took off down to the Awa. Maia stayed at the awa until dawn, when the Taniwha would change over, from day to night and from night to day.

"Hey, Taniwha, it's me," and they emerged with a flick of their tails.

The Taniwha noticed the greenstone taonga Maia was wearing.

"Where did you get that taonga from?"

"My Nanny Rakai gave it to me, and she received it from her Kuia."

"Many years ago, a Kuia wore that same taonga and promised my brother and me that she would send a Kaitiaki to release us from our fear. That Kaitiaki is you, Maia."

Maia was proud.

"My Kuia always says that if you want to find out about somebody, you need to go and see them—Kanohi ki te Kanohi and have a korero. I think the answer lies within the both of you."

The Taniwha looked at each other and then back at Maia.

"What do you mean?"

"Only darkness can take away the light, and only light can take away the darkness."

The brothers looked at each other and cried. They were able to help each other overcome their fears and bring day into night and night into day, and with a whip of their tails they thanked Maia and drifted into the depths of the awa. Maia headed back to his Nanny Rakai and gave her a huge hug.

Nanny Rakai looked at Maia and said, "thank you for being my Kaitiaki, my moko."

Maia looked at her and said, "No, Nanny, thank you for being mine."

Te Rau o Taku Patu

Cassiopeia Harrison

Nā wai rā, taku tūranga ake
Hōpara ki Whareponga
Whakamātauria ai ngā wai
Hotohoto kau ana ki tōku kiri e

Maumahara noa awau
Ki ngā rori kai puehu o te kāinga
Te ai o tōna rite, e kore ai e rite
Whanake ake taku Wīwī Nāti e

Rahuimanuka ki Mataahu
He kete aronui kāre i tua
E hika katuarehe mā
Hotuhotu te noho ki Pohatukura
He murimuri aroha i a au e

Hōake ki te wai ū o Roto a Tara
Whakatangata kia kaha e
Manawa rahi taku tū ki
Kahuranaki

Ko Rongokako i ōna tapuwae
Tāwhaiwhai nei

Tatū ai ki kauhanga riri
Hikohiko ko te rangi
Kōraha ko te whenua
Whatumoana te ao
I aku takahanga nei

He umu pōtaka ki te one
Raua atu aku ringa
Hei toto heke rā
Kaiākiri te ngau o tōku Paaka
Whakarukea ko Hikurangi e

Kengo ana te whiti
Maungarongo a pae maunga
Aumārire ko Orongonui
Whakarerea a huinga mahara e

Whale Brothers

R. de Wolf

A short story from R. de Wolf's novel, Brothers in Whalesong—Book Three of the Spirit Voyager Series. In Guardians of the Ancestors—Book One, heroine Marama is pregnant, and her unborn child forms a bond with a whale. The central characters of this story are Marama's eldest son Kai and his whale brother, Ira, who also appears in The Future Weavers—Book Two. You can find more information on the Spirit Voyager Series at www.rdewolf.com

The tide is calling my name, and my blood seems to run with the waves. It is time for me to depart. My younger siblings, Aroha and Maui, scrape flowing tears from their faces as they endeavour not to sob. I try to be brave for them and speak of the stories I will have to share when I return. When my mother Marama embraces me, I struggle to blink the moisture from my eyes.

"I know Ira will take care of you, Kai, and your fathers, but I'm your mother, and I love you. We will speak and think of you every day that you are gone."

My father comes to my rescue, slapping my back and telling me how proud of me he is. Of everyone, he alone understands the seductive call to voyage we experience as sons of the sea. He honours me with a hongi (touching noses) and nods his head at my waka (sailing canoe). Papa helped me build my voyaging waka, which I named Tūātea (wave crest), when the elders initiated me into manhood, so it is well seasoned for travel. The optimal time to launch arrives. I wave to my whanau (family) on the shore, and Ira shows off by splashing his tail, excited that I have returned to the ocean.

Tāwhirimātea (God of the Wind) teases the tears from my lashes as I hoist my sail to harness his breath. Although I am a son of the sea, I don't neglect any of the Gods. Complicated karakia (prayer and ritual) were completed with my parents and Aroha to curry favour with the Gods and ancestors. The waka is laden with so many blessings that I fear it might sink. I laugh out loud at my joke, and a playful wave slaps water in my face. The thrill of the journey ahead seizes me, and I whoop for joy as Ira breaches, inviting me to follow.

Ira is a humpback whale and he is magnificent. We connected when I was in Marama's womb, but Ira has grown ridiculously in the past few years. So have I, but my stature is puny in comparison to his. Our progress is swift. Even though we fish and play, when the wind blows in our direction, I ride on his back while he tows the waka.

"Are we in a hurry, Ira?" I ask. Although all our conversations occur in our minds, it is as easy as speaking.

"I need to arrive at our first destination at the right time, Kai. It wouldn't do for me to be late. What if I miss something important?"

Anxiety lurks behind his question, which is so unlike Ira. While I don't understand his sense of urgency, I share it. "You feel it too, don't you?" Ira asks.

"I can feel something, Ira, but I don't know what."

"We need to find mates, Kai. Our sea father gave us a task. Strong and enduring bloodlines won't create themselves, little brother—we need to get busy. I eat and grow larger to compete for the best mate to breed healthy calves. How are you planning to attract a mate? You are well past breeding age but haven't produced any young yet."

I attempt to explain to Ira that I have plenty of time to seek a mate, but in the end, I concede he has a point. Like my Papa before me, I attract many wāhine (women), but although I have dallied and enjoyed their attention, I never settle. Now that I think about it, I am one of the few men of my village, Kaingatīpu, my age who doesn't have children. Perhaps I am waiting to meet someone as unique as my mother.

"Don't wait for a Marama to find you. Your mother is one of a kind."

"I agree with you, Ira, but I want the mother of my children to be special. To accomplish our task, I need a mate who understands our world. She will be intelligent, sensitive, spiritual, fertile, with a sweet nature and beautiful, of course. What's so funny? I'm so glad I amuse you, big brother."

It seems Ira believes me a dreamer who has no understanding of the feminine psyche. He might be right, but I cling to the ideal I have envisaged as his laughter bubbles through me.

The sun deepens the colour of my skin at sea, and my hair bleaches to a streaky light brown. During the intense heat of the day, I shelter under my woven shade and nap, confident that Ira watches over me. When darkness descends, I search the stars and steer the course as the ancestral knowledge courses in my veins. My blood sings with joy, for I am in my element where I belong. I recall the story of my parents voyaging together and Papa teaching Mama to read the stars. Ira has baited my hook, and I find myself dreaming of sharing the wonders of the heavens with someone I love.

"See Kai, you want a mate as much as I do," Ira gloats.

As a voyager, I am grateful that l love the taste of fresh fish. The waka is laden with supplies from my mother, but Tangaroa (God of the Sea) blesses me with tuna and kingfish, which I fillet to eat raw and dipped in seawater. Like the dutiful son I am, I eventually eat my dried seaweed and smoked kumara as both my parents instructed me to do. I curl up to nap under a sun-filled sky with a full puku (belly).

The lurch of the waka wakes me. I can't feel Ira for the first time in days, and I cannot speak to him. We are disconnected. Whitecaps ride the choppy waves, and the sky is now an oppressive mass of angry clouds. I sniff the air and know a storm is brewing, but I also sense hostility and wonder where we are. While I slept, we may have strayed into the area where my people defeated their enemies on the way to Aotearoa. Ira is a colossal whale, but that doesn't stop me from worrying about him.

"Where are you, brother?" I call into the wind, but there is no response. The wind is building, gusty and malicious, so I pull down my sail before it's torn to shreds. My waka, Tūātea, tosses like a seed pod on the water, and I close my eyes to consider the available options.

Ride out the storm and hope the waves don't swamp my waka, try and run before the storm as Starman once did, or continue to search for Ira and hope he can lead us to safety swiftly?

A water spout spirals from the ocean to my right, then another to my left. Inside the spinning water, I glimpse a blur of ghoulish faces, and their ill-intent smacks me in the face as they grimace, anticipating revenge. Their shrill shrieking assaults my ears, and cold fingers brush my spine. But I am a son of the sea. My parents are Marama, Starman, and Tane the Brave, so I do not cower or flinch from these wasted souls.

"I belong to Tangaroa!" I shout in defiance. "You have no power over me. Go back where you belong."

The ghouls scream a discordant response. *"We demand utu (revenge) for our lost souls, you insolent calf. Together we will peel your flesh from your bones and devour you."*

The spouts move in on the waka, but I am chanting, calling on my ancestors, hands stretched to the sky. I implore my sea father to protect Ira so we may complete our task for him. Lightning cracks the sky, and the smell of ozone surrounds me as a bolt strikes the second water spout, collapsing it back into the ocean. The first spout is upon me and the prow of my waka lifts, sucked upwards by the revolving water. Thunderclaps and rumbles signal a warning to the ghouls, but they reach for me. I grab my whalebone mere. The weapon is made from the bones of Ira's tīpuna (ancestors) and imbued with many protective spells.

"Think you scare me dead things," I hiss, "we have defeated you twice before."

Perhaps it is risky to taunt them, but I have a true purpose, and they do not. An invisible heat source warms me. The sensation of the sun kissing my skin and aroha (love) burning fierce and bright. Tane shimmers next to me, his flaming taiaha (striking weapon) slicing impossible patterns through the air. On my left side, flanking me, is Nani Aroha, my great-grandmother. She cradles a stone bowl in her hands and blows glittering specks into the spiralling spout. I brandish my mere and strike the water. The ghouls are already screaming in pain as the spout dissipates in a cloud of spray. A hand reaches for me from the collapsing structure but evaporates under a double blow from my mere and Tane's taiaha.

My spirit father shimmers for a moment. His pride washes over me in radiant waves as he salutes Nani Aroha, and I feel so loved. The journey to the next realm no longer holds any fear because I have tasted the spirituality that awaits me. Finally, I understand my mother's explanation of her yearning to be reunited with Tane and her Nani. She told me about it because she considers it a flaw in her nature that I might have inherited. Now I know Marama is attracted to the divine, as any mere mortal would be.

Inspired karakia of thanks flow from my lips as if I have trained as a tohunga (spiritual expert) my whole life. My thoughts turn to my missing brother, so I open my skin and let my blood flow into the sea. I am worried that I still cannot sense Ira. The current takes my blood. Sharks circle but soon lose interest when there is no prey, but I follow the direction of the meandering thread.

"Tangaroa, our quest is unfulfilled. Please aid me in my search for Ira, my whale brother, for something is amiss."

The current takes the waka, and I hoist the sail again, imploring Tāwhirimātea to undo the mischief of his deceivers. Suddenly my waka stops. I peer over the side and perceive a large shape on the bottom of the seabed. The water is shallower here, so I anchor and dive in, making for the shadow below.

It is Ira, but he is just lying there. He needs to breathe just as I do and I am concerned we have been disconnected for so long. I am desperate to wake him up, but he is unresponsive. Swimming to the surface to breathe, I try to come up with a plan to stir him. Tane's flaming taiaha appears in my mind, so I clamber aboard the waka and unwrap my prized weapon. The taiaha was made for me by an artisan of consummate skill. While I am reluctant to take such a fine weapon into the sea, it might be the only way to save Ira. I rub the weapon with an extra coating of fat to protect the wood before I suck in as much air as possible and dive to the seafloor. Leaning into the taiaha, I place the sharp blade against a soft part of Ira's skin, trying to cause enough pain to get a reaction. He still doesn't move, and I swallow my panic. His eyes are robust, so I decide to poke his bum. It isn't dignified, but I don't want to damage his dorsal fin, and I already tried biting his mouth. I pray to everyone that he won't poop on me.

Causing Ira pain is something I never expected to do, but his life depends on me. My throat constricts and tears well. "Please," I plead silently, "I cannot lose my brother."

Whether my sea father answered my prayer or my lack of air created a link between us, I feel Ira. Kicking for the surface to breathe, I scream at Ira in my head to surface. I share the taste of salty air in my lungs, my relief at breathing and finally, he stirs. Diving down and swimming to his eye, I signal Ira to come up with me. He is sluggish, but our connection holds, so I recite a mantra, "swim to the air," to try and move him. Ira lumbers through the water, lacking his usual grace of movement. When he breaks the surface, Ira breathes and becomes more alert. My relief swamps him, and he teases me.

"Ah! So, you do love me."

"Of course, I do, you lump of blubber!" My tears of relief and snotty nose underscore my declaration of love.

"Ow, my bum hurts," he moans.

"Sorry, Ira, but that was how I woke you up because I ran out of options. Forgive me?"

"I'll think about it," he jokes. "What happened, Kai?"

"The spirits who assailed us possess a powerful sleep enchantment. These are the same ghouls who tried to kill my mother when our people fled to Aotearoa. My grandmother and tīpuna wove many protections around Marama and me while I was in her womb. It is the reason I was less affected than you. We must give thanks to them and our sea father. If it wasn't for their efforts, I might have lost you." My voice breaks with emotion.

"Well, perhaps I forgive you, after all, little brother. Let's sing a song of gratitude together."

I clamber atop Ira's hulking form and lay flat against him while we sing. The contact with Ira comforts me, and I am grateful because the separation has left me shaken.

When the stars come out, I triangulate the location of the foul spirits, determined to avoid ever passing there again.

I hoist my sail. Destiny calls us, and Ira and I have a quest to fulfil.

The Hollow Mother

R. de Wolf

It was a Saturday night, and the fundraiser dance for the rugby team at Uepohatu in Ruatorea was starting to hum. Eighteen-year-old Puti Taylor was a beauty with an enchanting smile. A glint of light on freshly-fallen snow when Hikurangi greets the dawn. Her nubile body was poetry in rhythm on the dance floor.

Already promised in marriage by her parents to a 'wonderful man'—their words, not hers—Puti was dizzy with excitement at a breath of freedom.

Eyes locked, heart skipped, love at first sight. Aue! What to do? Thomas Kepa didn't hesitate. He swept Puti into his arms and rocked her round the clock before devouring an innocent heart for supper with his beer. A nervous Puti fretted about what her parents might say, but she had read books and poems about the power of love. Surrendering to Thomas' charm, they consummated their passion on the back seat of his car.

Nausea bubbled from Puti's stomach to her throat. She vomited her porridge into the long-drop. Spittle clung to her chin as she pushed the back door open. The stinging clap of her mother's hand connecting with her cheek startled her, and tears invited themselves to her eyes.

"You will marry Henry. Tomo marriage is our way, and you will not disgrace our family. Do you hear me!"

"But Mama, I love Thomas, and he loves me," sobbed Puti. "We could raise our baby together, be a family."

"Are you stupid? Thomas Kepa loves every woman who opens her legs for him. I thought we raised you better than that. He is a cad Puti, and he is already married to a drunken wife and has six snot-nosed brats."

Mouth hanging open in disbelief, Puti's dreams collapsed in an ugly heap. She sank to the floor, cradling her spinning head in her hands and sobbed.

The Service Car indicator flashes its intention to journey to Wellington. The battered family suitcase is stowed in the hold with tiny clothes for the newborn. Puti has never been anywhere by herself, and her enormous puku shrinks her seat. A dour nun meets her at the station and takes her straight to the hospital even though Puti is hungry and thirsty. Brusque nursing staff jab a needle in her arm.

"If your waters break, or you start contractions, ring the bell." The nurse left Puti alone in a sterile room with the curtain drawn to shield her shame from prying eyes. The girl had no idea what the nurse was talking about; nobody had told her what to expect. Before her puku became noticeable, her parents sent her to an isolated farm, where she worked for her board while everyone ignored her.

Puti screamed as the pain tore through her body.

"Am I dying?" she wailed.

"Be quiet. Bite down on this; you are giving birth."

Legs dangle above in stirrups—no modesty in this place. A gowned doctor pokes, prods, and tells Puti to be still as dead eyes rake her private parts. The excruciating contractions ruling her body shove her shame into the corner. Cold forceps force their way inside her, and Puti screams again as her heart hammers in her breast. Surely, I must die soon, she thinks, and Puti wonders if death will be painless. With a final push of contractions and a yank from the doctor's forceps, the baby shoots into the world—dripping, purple, and still attached by his umbilical cord. The maternity team clean up efficiently. There are no congratulations or kind words for Puti.

"Can I hold him?" Puti croaks.

Nobody responds to her question. Aunty Pearl and Uncle Jack have arrived from Taranaki. They lift the baby, now swaddled in blankets.

"It will be best for you and him if you don't see each other."

Aunty Pearl's words aren't unkind, but they rip Puti to pieces. The tap of their departing shoes on the hospital lino is morse code for 'you have lost your son.'

Mrs Taylor is delighted with the wedding. Henry looks dashing, and although Puti is still dumpy from her pregnancy, they have squeezed her into a corset and modest dress. Puti cements the family obligations and the bond to Henry's whanau and whenua (land). A pale shadow of the vivacious girl she was is reflected in Puti's mirror, as the dull ache of her lost child persists, like time itself.

A devoted mother and wife, Puti and Henry produce three children. They go to school with homebaked bread, cakes, and fruit from the yard in their lunchboxes. After she waves goodbye to the school bus, Puti climbs on a stool and coaxes the cooking sherry from the pantry's top shelf. Henry loves her sherry trifle. All alone, she drinks. And while she drinks, Puti mourns the loss of love, innocence, youth, but most of all, her first child.

'As women, we think we struggle for equality now, and we do, but not so long ago, men utterly dominated the world—a glimmer of hope that our 'snail' is still in the progress race.'

The Boat on the Sea

Holly Flyger

A little boat sits on the ocean.
It sits there in all conditions,
when dark and cataclysmic waves threaten to tear the boat apart,
when still and sunny conditions provide the perfect opportunity
for moving on.

Rain or shine the boat's in its position,
because the ship's scared to move.
Going into deeper waters means it's further to fall.
Heading back towards shore means losing the progress
already made.

As time passes the boat stays still.
Allowing other boats to pass by.
Never venturing away in case that proves fatal.
Until algae and rot besiege the boat's exterior and it sinks
to the bottom.

Sailing Panama Ends in Military Escort

Vicki Cosson

"A man, a plan, a canal, Panama."
One of the world's most famous palindromes, written by Lee Mercer

Panama's area is 74,177.3 km sq (NZ is 3.6 times the size, according to madaboutpanama.com). Their population is 4,052,481 with nearly half living in the capital, Panama City. For those geographically challenged, Panama is the isthmus between North and South America. The Panama Canal arrangement is essentially three locks from the Atlantic or Caribbean side. Water fills in and we're going up three levels, into the Gatun Lake, that meanders across the width of Panama. The last three locks heading into the Pacific go down three levels.

July

The week of preparations for the transit disappeared very quickly with paperwork, bank deposits, grocery provisioning, refuelling and filling water tanks. But soon, Canal Day arrived. Our lines and fenders (old tyres) had been delivered, our line-handlers had arrived and so had a rather large crew of friends to see us off. I tried to start the engine, checked the switches, tried again: nothing.

"Um, Dave, can you take a look at this?" I asked my husband.

There was so much noise from the kids, no-one noticed my concern. Dave fiddled about, managed to get it in the correct sweet spot and fired the engine to life. Meandering out at snail pace, the poor marina occupants listened to constant good-byes from the kids ashore, running about the finger slips, following us out! We motored a short distance, half hour or so, to the industrial side of Colon to the "flats" anchorage where we waited for our pilot to be delivered by boat. Every boat is required to hire a pilot who carries a vhf, and is the contact liaison between Canal authorities, pilot boats and ships, giving instructions as to timing and which path to take enroute. Boat owners are advised to feed and hydrate the pilots and line handlers for the duration of the transit.

At 4.30 pm our pilot arrived. Upon his command, I was to come up alongside the catamaran we'd been following, in order to tie up with them. This was mid canal entrance, with wakes of the constant shipping and pilot boat traffic bouncing us. Taking into consideration wind and current effects, I slowly tried to aim our aluminium, gaff rigged schooner, sometimes referred to by visitors as a 'tank,' along with her overbearing bowsprit towards the glitzy catamaran filled over with mostly rotund, retirement-aged American tourists waltzing around in their bathing suits, watching our every move.

I was trying desperately to get close enough for them to catch lines without scraping our bowsprit along the length of their shiny boat, feeling the pressure as all eyes were on us.

Meanwhile, there's a constant chatter near me that will not stop. Right in my ear, it's my five-year-old: "Mum, do you remember that movie, where that guy had that thing, with that other guy and they were going to go do that thing ... at that place? Do you remember what that movie was?" (Or something to that effect, equally as random.)

"Ugh!! Really not a good time Eden!"

Tied up successfully, we motored conjointly into the first lock, following one of the ships that had just passed us. A huge tug snuggled in behind us.

The monkey fists, (rope tied into a cool looking knot), got thrown to us from the men on the walls, which we then attached to our lines, threw them back ashore so both ends were tied down. An alarm went off, and the massive iron doors closed at either end and the water started to churn into the chamber.

As we rose, the ropes holding us in place had to be constantly adjusted at our bollards. Once at the top, the lock doors open. The men on land pulled us along with ropes, having to climb a steep set of stairs to reach the next chamber. The ship's ropes were then attached to what could best be described as trains pulling them along.

During this time, the catamaran was driving the two of us, still tied alongside together, while I adjusted the throttle according to the advisor's directions. While sitting at the helm, I noticed out the window, Dave's legs at the edge of the boat, and on the other boat, many sets of legs, all milling around Dave, he seemed to have become the star attraction! They were asking lots of questions about what we were doing. Did we have a generator? (no) and a water maker? (no), they'd look at the paint flaking off the decks and say, "oh, yes, it does need a bit of work!" The group were chartering the boat, with a young Aussie Captain and Kiwi stewardess couple taking them through. One of the tourists promptly came out with souvenir t-shirts for Dave and I.

The next two locks were thankfully fairly uneventful, but also very enjoyable. Once out of the last lock, we untied, motored about 20 minutes into the Gatun Lake and grabbed a mooring, where our advisor skilfully jumped ship onto a pilot boat to go home. Our line handlers stayed on for the night, having dinner pre-made, we enjoyed the sunset, drinks and semi-conversations of mixed Spanish and English.

It was hot and muggy and the lake was very alluring, but the many croc stories discouraged us from indulging. Admittedly, I did end up having a quick dip early morning to freshen up!

Up early, preparing apple yoghurt muesli the next morning, expecting the advisor to arrive at 7.30 am, it was 9.30 am by the time we left, due to some delay in the canal.

The catamaran had left about an hour before, which ended up working in our favour: we got to take the more scenic "banana cut," shaving off about a half hour or so between mangroves and islands.

We were praying it wouldn't rain for our canal transit, mostly out of concern of visibility. A tall order in Panama, during monsoon season, where thunderstorms are a daily occurrence. It did rain ... actually, it poured. But I could see anywhere between two and five markers ahead, which was enough. There was some pretty intense thunder and lightning overhead, a major concern for all sailors as the lightning can wipe out all electronics. Every sailor we met in Panama had either been struck, or knew someone who had, it was that prevalent.

We found out later that because of the lack of visibility, the large ship behind had to ease right back, which actually set us up better for the next set of locks, which allowed us to catch up with the catamaran and tied alongside them again. They cheered and clapped.

I suddenly felt rather teary, the reality of all our years of planning and hard work had actually brought us from the far side of the Caribbean to the Pacific. We almost had our boat on the right side of the world at long last! While waiting for a large ship behind to get set up and meet us in the lock, I was also very fortunate to have constant communication with family on WhatsApp, as they watched us through cameras online. Further adding to the rather surreal experience, they would send us pics of them watching us, a tiny little boat slowly manoeuvres through the lock system.

Watching our depth sounder, we were at seventy-five feet at the first lock, then dropped down to about fifty-four feet, as the water went out. The gates opened and by the time we reached the next lock gate, we were at seventy-five feet again! The water going out of these locks was very subtle. We motored out of the last lock, untied from the catamaran, then followed the buoys out of the busy harbour and under the bridge of the Americas - joining South America to Central and North America.

Our advisor kindly complimented me on doing a good job before leaving on his pilot boat ride.

We were in the Pacific!

August

After many provisioning trips, major outfitting etc we were preparing for the Pacific crossing, some 4,000 miles of open ocean, with first stop being Marquesas Islands, French Polynesia.

We had allotted the boys an evening time slot each for the watches, with either Dave or I dozing in the cockpit with them. They knew what was expected of them, including filling in the log book, checking on bilges, engine gauges, wind direction, course direction and, of course, traffic. They took their job seriously and it enabled Dave and I to get longer stints of sleep.

I enjoy getting into the rhythm of passages and night watches, having the time to myself to read, write, exercise a little and watch the conditions outside. It takes me quite a few days to get over the nauseous/zombie mode, so nothing much is done unless it's absolutely necessary, including meals (I try to have a couple already made before leaving). Things are pretty basic.

We were keeping in touch with our friends on another yacht, the *S/V Rosanna* on a daily basis, who had left a week before us. We both had the same satellite tracking device, not too dissimilar to a cell phone allowing us to text each other. It was a great moral boost and we were plotting their course on our paper chart to get an idea of their track. We had two other navigational digital charts between our tablet and phone, plus the GPS on our sat phone that was also sending out our track to a website our friends and family could watch back home.

Ten days at sea brought about some unexpected circumstances however, and we had to make the difficult decision to return to Panama and sell.

We had hoped to make landfall for our sons' eleventh birthday, but due to the light winds, we were still another day away from the nearest island. He had such a great attitude and actually relished the fact that not many people get to say they spent their birthday in the Pacific Ocean. The Gulf of Panama, no less.

Salem received a much-desired Hawaiian sling, some birthday cards from his brothers and our friends on *S/V Bonaire*, who had sneakily provided me with a little package of goodies before we left. Salem's good attitude was well rewarded with some interesting occurrences: we were entertained by a swordfish jumping out of the water multiple times; a bright yellow bird landed on the lifeline next to us in the cockpit, scooted along closer to us, then flew through the cockpit, landing on my plate for a bit, then flew up on top of my head for a while before finally taking off again (Hmm, perhaps it's time I did something with my nest-like hair!) Topped off by the ultimate ending—a soft glowing sunset with our landfall in sight, was met with a huge pod of hundreds of dolphins, as far as the eye could see, doing all sorts of acrobatics and squeaking away.

What we thought could potentially be a boring birthday turned out to be one that would be hard to beat.

September

We dropped anchor for the first time in twelve days at the private island San Jose, with an idyllic long, white sand beach backed with green foliage and coconut trees to greet us. As soon as we dinghied ashore, the two younger boys dashed to the river running out into the ocean, where they began to build a dam and ride the fast-flowing current down on their bellies or boogie boards.

We enjoyed putting our legs to more use, found some large holes in the sand where turtles had obviously been to lay their eggs and cracked open oysters in the hope of finding a pearl, being in 'Las Perlas' (Pearl Islands).

We found out about the famous pearl from these islands, called La *Peregrina*. The story goes that the pearl was originally found by an African slave and was 'given' to Don Pedro de Temez, the administrator of the Spanish colony in Panama. The slave who found it was rewarded with freedom. The pearl was carried to Spain and given by Temez to the future Phillip II of Spain, who in turn gifted *La Peregrina* to Mary I of England in anticipation of their marriage.

After her death in 1558, the pearl was returned to the Crown of Spain for the next two hundred and fifty years. In 1808, the elder brother of Napoleon, Joseph Bonaparte, was installed as King of Spain. When he was forced to leave five years later, he took among other things, *La Peregrina*. When he died, as stated in his will, the pearl was left to his nephew, the future Napoleon III of France. During Napoleon's exile in England, the Emperor sold it and eventually it came into the hands of the Duke of Abercorn.

His family owned the *Pearl* until 1969 when they put it up for auction at Sotheby's in London, where Richard Burton purchased *La Peregrina* for $37,000, giving it to his wife, Elizabeth Taylor, as a Valentine's Day gift during their first year of marriage. At one stage, the pearl went missing, but later discovered that one of the actor's dogs had been chomping on it. There's some debate as to how it was found, or more importantly, from what end of the canine! Taylor commissioned Cartier to redesign a necklace with *La Peregrina* taking centre stage.

In December 2011 La Peregrina sold for a record price of more than $11 million!!

The sun hadn't even got out of bed the next morning when we heard a "lancha" (long, open wooden dinghy, usually powered by three large outboards) pull up alongside us. Someone was yelling right outside our bedroom ports,

"*Ula, Ula*!" (The name of our vessel).

It took us a while to wake from our dead sleep, the first full night in sometime, and stumble out with slightly more appropriate clothing for visitors. We were greeted by five large military men, AK47's and other such weapons attached.

Our cruising guide said that in spite of the island being private, it was fine to anchor and explore ashore. My confused look prompted the man leading our armed guests, to explain some more. We need to leave now because a bomb will be going off in a couple of hours ashore and we couldn't stay there. Dave figured it must be a commonly deployed mosquito bomb to keep all the flying annoyances at a minimum, being a private island.

There was a slight hitch however. We couldn't move. The previous night, we had filtered through some diesel between tanks and were planning to bleed the lines that morning. There was no chance our engine would start without us going through this lengthy procedure. Out came our 'Spanish for Cruisers Guide' and I frantically looked for the explanation to convey to the impatient military guys. This led us to a very impatient officer jumping on deck, helping Dave with the manual anchor winch system, while the other guys set up ropes from their "lancha" and before we knew it, we were being towed at 5.6 knots, the fastest Ula had done in months!

Along the way, Dave queried the Superior about the *bomba.*

"Mosquito?" he asked.

"No, chemical bomb," the man answered.

"For mosquito?" Dave asked again.

To which the reply was a gesture made of a hand slicing through the neck. "No, chemica." He proceeded, in his broken English and our very limited Spanish, to enlighten us on the situation ...

In the 1960's the Americans decided to trial a chemical bomb, intended for the Vietnam war, but it never went off. Today, of all days, the US military were there to safely dispose of the bomb and they needed a three-mile radius!! The bonus to all this was that they towed us to an even better spot than before to set anchor.

Having explored ashore and bled our lines allowing us to once again motor, due to no wind, we felt compelled to continue onto the next island of *Pedro Gonzales*. Ensuring an extra three-mile-wide gap or more was between us and *San Jose*, we cruised along and were met in the late afternoon by the most wonderful surprise: a yacht was in the anchorage. Not only that, as we neared, we discovered it was in fact our good friends from *S/V Bonaire*! They welcomed us back from our Pacific ordeal, with warm encouragement, as they paddled over to us by kayak!

During the next week or so the two boat kids met regularly after school work and chores. They explored, swam, paddled, played football, snorkelled, saw lots of stingrays, dug holes etc. Emily and I got into the wonderful routine of an early morning swim ashore, walking the length of the beach, while hoarding more treasures of shells and stones (much to our husbands' disdain), then a return swim back to our boats. One morning we even discovered mama turtle tracks going up the beach, and returning back down to the sea. Under the branch of a tree where the two tracks met was a rounded, scuffed up area where we presumed the mother must have laid her eggs before returning.

It was a much-needed reprieve, but before long, the restlessness was mounting, knowing it was time to get back to civilisation, and Internet.

It was time to sell our home, Ula.

So many years of reading about other couples and families living the sailing life, I always felt sad when they decided to sell up and settle on land. Yet here I was facing the reality that it was also my story.

The adjustment took some time, and to be honest, it still is. I find living in a house with its constant bills, shut off from nature and its inability to move places; the everyday routine of land life to be rather claustrophobic. I know I have a lot to be grateful for, especially the easy, beautiful country we're so blessed to call home.

It will be nice to be able to relax a bit more. We had some fun, saw and experienced unforgettable places and people. Now it's time to let this boat go and find a new adventure.

Light Keeper

Philomena McGann

Watch the shine in love's eyes
Spy the warmth reverberating
Glance at devotion in the skies
The firmament encasing
Prickles of light in darkest night
Echo loves sound from the day
Trees bend in homage
Waft in the breeze
Flowers and birdlife display
Gaze at a leaf as it slowly uncurls
Green is its pleasure to gift us
The brook that is weaving
A lake lit in evening

The ocean breaks and roars
In the storm of your life
Yet gifts calm at its ebb
Flows love in its stead
And we
Keep breathing

Book of Firsts

Susan Partington

The heater in his old car struggled to keep out the chill so they still wore their coats. When he suggested a drive out to the lake after dinner, Holly thought this was code for park and make out. After all, it was too dark to see the water and too cold to get out of the car. Not that there was much to see anyway, it was one of those man-made reservoirs dotted across the American plains, with a dam on one side and walking tracks for the baby boomers on the other. This is it, she thought, this is going to be my first real kiss. She supposed she was a late bloomer, seventeen and never been kissed. Her mom was pregnant at her age.

Holly was surprised when Lucas asked her out to dinner because she thought she was firmly in the friend zone. She'd never really had feelings for him, but she liked his quirky jokes and he dressed better than most guys in her class.

He pulled onto the gravel road, away from the suburban street lights and neighbourly porch lights, into pitch darkness. Heavy clouds hid the moon. The trees closed in around the car and made her more aware of Lucas' elbow almost touching hers on the console, the warm bulk of his body next to her. Since she was used to having a cafeteria table between them or seeing him across the hallway, this proximity felt intimate.

This would make a good entry into the 'Book of Firsts,' an old notebook her friends started years ago at a slumber party where they recorded memorable firsts. It was a simple spiral notebook with a tattered cover, thick with doodles. This book was started in middle school before they all had smartphones and could communicate with each other often and instantly. Now the 'Book of Firsts' felt like a hallowed item from the past, a revered written history of the ups and downs of their teenage lives. They had vowed to complete honesty, everything went in the book, but the secret Holly carried still felt too heavy to put into words.

A four-colour pen was jammed into the spiral, and all entries were colour coded by theme. Blue ink was for any first relating to romance. A few years ago, these entries were about kissing and handholding, but had gotten racier over time, such as a recent entry from Jude: *First time my sister walked in on me and Todd doing the deed. Getting a lock for my door ASAP!* Black ink was for dark emotions - sadness, depression, anger: First birthday since Dad moved out. The only upside was I got two cakes. Red ink was for anything period related: *First period stain at school. Thanks for letting me borrow your hoodie, Jenna!* Green used to be for vomit stories, but since Jenna's whole bulimia thing last year, green changed to gratitude. Personally, Holly found these posts a bit dull: *So grateful I have the best friends ever. LUV YOU!* But occasionally funny ones came through: *I'm grateful I don't have cankles like Jessica Jeffries.* This night might lead to her first time clicking the blue ink into place.

"So do you come here often?" she said, hoping her jokey tone masked the awkwardness of the line.

"My dad and I fish here all the time," he answered sincerely. She felt better knowing that this dark maze of dirt roads was familiar to him and that his answer didn't involve another girl.

The headlights of an oncoming pickup truck lit up the interior of the car briefly, and she saw Lucas in profile—strong jaw, floppy hair, hands firmly at ten and two. She imagined that face leaning towards hers. In preparation for tonight, Jude had given her tips on kissing. Apparently, everyone tilted their heads to the right whilst kissing and the lips should be slightly parted, not tight. Jude had kissed lots of guys, like nearly double digits.

"There's a spot just around the corner where we can park," Lucas said. Yes, this is definitely happening, she thought, hoping her breath smelled decent. Jude had told her to avoid garlic bread.

As they turned the corner, the arc of the headlights flashed upon two large lumps in the road. They were unmistakably human, bulky in winter coats and the white soles of four shoes were all lined up across the road, toes down in the mud. The moment was thrown into sharp focus, as she thought, *those are dead people*. It was the same danger instinct that caused humans instantly to see a snake slide through the leaf litter or a gun gleaming in a crowd. Her heart beat loud and wet in her chest, as if to remind her of the exquisite vitality she'd taken for granted all these years.

She heard her own voice, high and trembling, say, "those are dead people," but had no awareness of forming the words.

Lucas hit the brakes, sending up a fine mist of dust swirling in the beams from the headlights, obscuring the alarming sight. "Um, maybe it's an animal. Or something else ..."

"What else could it be? Those are dead people. I see their shoes." Holly's words caught in her throat as tears sprang instantly to her eyes. Her German teacher, Herr Busch, had taught them a phrase that translated to "built close to the water" to describe emotional people. She couldn't remember the German, but she felt she was always close to water, a wide pool located just out her back door whose still water was opaque and immeasurably deep. At this moment, she felt close to drowning.

Frantically throwing the car into reverse and twisting around in his seat, Lucas said, "we have to get out of here." But the car seemed to get tangled in the low tree branches that surrounded them, and it took him a few tries to reverse the car back far enough so that the bodies in the road were no longer spot lit by his car.

"Were those really dead people? How did they get there?" He noticed her tears, silently flowing down her face. "Are you ok?"

"Yeah, I'm ok. What do we do? Call the police, right?" she said while taking quick gulps of air. She wiped her tears on her sleeve as she dug through her bag for her phone.

He pulled out his phone and turned off the radio. "Hey, I'll make the call. You can hardly speak." He was eager to do something constructive and competent after the mess he made trying to reverse the car. When they asked which emergency service was needed, he wavered between ambulance and police, but his gut told him this was murder, not a medical emergency.

"Police, please. Yes, we're at Lake Sheldon, the east side near the jetty. There are two people ... bodies. We think they're dead." He paused. "No, just us. Um, they were laying down. I don't know. It's really dark. Okay, bye." He looked over at Holly, "They're coming. They want us to meet them back on the main road."

"Why?" she asked, then realized with a jolt that their safety was at stake. This was a crime scene. "Okay, let's get out of here. Do you know the way?"

The road was just wide enough for him to turn around, and they drove back to the main road in nervous silence. As they pulled up under the street light, four police cruisers arrived with flashing lights but no sirens, and cops swarmed out of the cars. A young officer walked towards them with the air of someone who'd drawn the short straw. "Good evening." This greeting struck Holly as condescending despite its old-world charm.

"Hello, Officer." Lucas had somehow become their spokesperson for which she was grateful. Her body was shivering with the cold and shock, and she hated this role of crying, helpless female she'd cast herself in. When asked, he gave their names "Lucas Stevens and Holly Hendricks, sir," in a calm, confident tone she envied.

She was thankful when the officer told her she could sit in the back of the nearest cruiser. The hum of the engine and the blast of heat finally made her feel safe. Another officer handed her a form on a clipboard and asked her to write a statement. "Just write everything you saw. No detail is too small." Her writing looked large and childish to her when she handed it back. This was the first real interaction she'd had with the police, first time in a police car. She'd choose black ink for this entry in the "Book of Firsts."

She worried and waited, listening to the unintelligible crackle of the radio until the door opened and Lucas got in the car next to her. "Thank Christ it's warm in here."

"Where did they take you? Did you write a statement? Did you tell them about that white pickup truck we saw?" she asked, her crying thankfully stopped and her breathing regular again.

"I thought it was a red truck. I showed them the spot and then wrote a statement. They said to wait in here, and then I can take you home." He took her hand across the back seat, "Are you okay? You seemed really upset."

"I'm alright. Are we suspects?" she'd been imagining herself wrongly accused of murder, a wasted life in prison.

"No way. They know we were kids who were in the wrong place at the wrong time. They were nice guys actually, joking about us coming to the lake to make out," he grinned, and she relaxed a little, feeling comfortably close to Lucas.

Shocked by her own boldness, she leaned slightly towards his face illuminated in flashes of red and blue. "Can I kiss you?"

"Hey, I really like you, but no. I don't think it's a good idea."

As she pulled back, her traitorous tears gave away her disappointment instantly. "It's not you, I promise." He sounded sincere but she was still confused. "Why did we come parking at the lake if you're not into me?"

"I wanted to show you the Pleiades, the constellation called the Seven Sisters. You can see it really well without the light pollution."

"Stargazing ... you brought me out here to look at the stars," she laughed through her tears. "I thought we were going to make out."

Lucas bit his lip. "I'm sorry I led you on, but here's the thing. I'm gay. I never told anybody before."

"So why did you ask me out?" she asked while realizing that perhaps she'd built it up in her mind as a date, but maybe he just considered it hanging out with a friend.

"I'm not totally sure to be honest. I like you as a friend, and the guys were pressuring me to go out with someone. So, I thought I'd give it a try. But deep down, I know I like guys. There. I've said it."

She felt the truth of the statement. In fact, she and her friends had joked that Lucas might be gay, because of his style and sensitivity. No other guy at their school wore a thumb ring. She now felt ashamed of these jokes, despite their accuracy. She reached across and took his other hand, which felt easy now since she knew the truth. "That's cool. Your secret is safe with me."

He smiled and squeezed her hands. "Now you have to tell me a secret," he said. "Something you've never told anyone." The secret she'd been living with for weeks popped into her mind. On this surreal evening in the dim confessional of the police car, the secret bubbled to the surface.

"You know those DNA tests you can do? Well, I took one to find out who my bio father is. My mother would never tell me who the guy was, I'm not even sure she knows," she said, relieved to say the words she'd been holding in. The subject of her father was taboo in her house. She'd overheard her mom refer to him once as 'the sperm donor' over a bottle of wine with friends, but her mom never mentioned him to Holly. As soon as she'd saved enough money from her after-school job, she'd ordered the test online without her mom's knowledge. "Well, I found out who it is, and it's someone I know. He teaches at our school."

Her hands shook when she first opened the email with the results. Derek James Busch was a 98% match for her biological father. She quickly googled him and was stunned to see the face of her German teacher pop up, with his eyes as dark as hers. She'd never noticed his eye colour before. She'd never thought about him before. He was just part of the scenery of the school—like the flagpole or the beige carpet—something she'd passed everyday but never really noticed, aside from the embarrassing time he'd worn lederhosen to the class Oktoberfest.

She had thought about telling her friends or confronting her mom, but she had held on to the secret, like a warm marble in her pocket. Finding out who her bio dad was had changed everything, but also nothing at all.

"Who? I mean, you don't have to tell me if you don't want to ..." he paused.

"It's Herr Busch. He's been my teacher for two years. I can't believe he's my dad. I don't even know if he knows."

"Oh, Coach Busch. He was my wrestling coach." She burned with shame as she remembered watching his wrestling meet and her friends making snide comments about the wrestlers looking gay as they grappled in their spandex suits.

"It feels good to tell someone. I just didn't think it'd be someone I know. I thought it would be a stranger I'd have to track down, not someone I see every third period."

He started laughing. "What's so funny?" she asked nervously, worried that she'd revealed too much.

"I just realized if he's your dad, your name would be Holly Busch!" This struck them both as absolutely hilarious, and they burst into a fit of laughter that was more than the joke deserved, but felt like a necessary relief after the tension of the evening. After a few minutes, the laughter would die down and then one of them would snicker and they would start all over again, until the policeman opened the car door and told them they were free to go. As they climbed out of the cop car, the moon slid out from behind the clouds, so buoyant and bright that their shadows bounded across the silver road and they felt extravagantly alive.

Basket Weaver

Katrina Reedy

Elaine lived in the suburbs,
With strong back she worked hard
nurturing, as her children grew
in vital soils, sand, sea and sky
Eager hands had she,
always something to do
her DNA compels her,

Use your hands!

So she tried her hand at all sorts
In her blood, the drive create
to provide warmth, water, shelter
even with kai ~ she wove in
all that was available

There is no stopping the imprint of
ancients who pulled green-lipped edge
Along evenly prepared flax lengths
Hear the long ago scraping revealing

heartstrings the colour of 'waiū'
as light as air.

In the way of her colonial town
Elaine spent her coin at Muirs cycles
bought circular bases, pliers, patterns
bundles of cane, modern dyes
rattan lengths, both round and flat
She carried them home on nifty fifty
Soaked her materials, long, in a bath
of deep purple Condy's crystalline water
Exotics emerged, rich brown, supple, ready

At sunset,
after work,
she wove twins,
jovial characters
with ample belly
A gift set for a friend
to fill with life
after loss.

This was her way
Elaine was a skilled maker.
A weaver of Alibaba baskets.

Tears of before and after fall
Before her moko turned one
Elaine passed away
too soon,
before
the internet

online learning
polytech classes
had a chance to open
the way back to
pūkenga raranga harakeke...

A small matter, not knowing flax
intimately, that didn't stop Elaine
she wove anyway...

Nō reira kua wātea te ara

for her mokopuna,
to be flax weavers...

eagerly
harakeke mokopuna
reach sunward,
a harvesting
of lush flax lengths
when the time is right

Her Hands

Katrina Reedy

for us mokopuna there was only one
nanna banna, my mum's mum

Tauatoru Mairia Ngaira Poi

and boy
her hands
oh her hands...
they were mothering hands
big and swollen and warm and smooth
hands that fed nourishing milk to her premature brother
that cut wood for a winter of lifegiving fires
that helped birth babies
that reared her own babies
and welcomed whangai with
open kindness
they were
hands that, heartbreakingly
buried her own babies too
they were

hands that fed masses of visitors
to Bulli Street
hands that cable knit cardigans and jerseys
and crocheted doilies and bread bag hats
hands that scrubbed and mopped floors
and unblocked sinks
that wallpapered kitchens
and hallways and bedrooms
and got dirty socks
pearly white
with just
sunlight soap
and a good scrub
I tried it once
I couldn't even get them near white!
nanna's hands
cleaned and cleaned and cleaned
and folded and folded and folded us
into a tight-knit extended whanau
they were
hands that rose before dawn
to cook mutton stew
for shepherds around a campfire
and laboured day in day out
at *Wattie's Cannery*
they were
hands that made curried sausages stretch
across all the mokopuna mouths every afternoon
while sons and daughters were at work
they were
hands that harvested sweet figs
avocado and apple cucumber

that collected feijoas, tangelos
white fleshed nectarines,
golden queen peaches
purple potatoes, kumara
and lemons from
grandpas famous lemon tree
nanna's hands
peeled and peeled and peeled
and at times
they literally peeled away the cold
from shivering mokopuna
with loooooong nanna hugs
yet it wasn't all work and no play
around midday each day
hands rested
as nanna watched *Young and the Restless*
and the scandalous *Days of Our Lives.*
and wouldn't you know it
sometimes those
hands dipped
into her kete to get us lollies
usually blackballs
sometimes raspberry drops
and most importantly to me
they were
hands that made lemon drink
with arataki honey
that kept a check on feverish temperatures
smoothed the brow when mokopuna got sick
and applied a cool cloth to a burning forehead
they were
hands that pulled mattresses

into the sitting room
so we could all sleep with nanna banna
on the floor in front of the TV
They were those
Hands, those mesmerising
Hands that warmed
causing little eyes to finally get sleepy
and when we mokopuna left home
they were
hands that wrote to us
in a distinctive recognisable hand
and we each have her letters to this day
they were our nans hands
never hands that touched a drink
never hands that touched a cigarette
never ever hands that hit
only ever hands that nurtured
they were
hands I do not have
hands I aspire to having
Hands we miss now they are gone.

He waiata i te oro a ika

(A song in the key of ika)

Katrina Reedy

pūrākau pūtaiao
me pao, me kī!

story I implore
download to us

pakeke fishing secrets
on river & shore

of aka
bone
of sharp shell
stone

of toki
say free

how they intricately
wove hinaki

shaped hei matau
used sharp tool

& sharper wit
to fish up our land

to nourish
so we may flourish

Tuna

Katrina Reedy

Mātaotao enei waimārino
here where the river branches
ki konei ki tenei manga-a-awa
On this curve of this river
shimmying with swerve
eels fat and shiny,
move silkily
i ro' wai,
overstone,
underbelly,
overspine,
twist and
entwine,
writhe and
dance!
Keepers of your corner
nature's gauge of river health
It is we, whom you sustain
tuna, e kori nei
may you

have the
stealth
to evade our rama,
to live another day
and when it comes...
May the light shining
in the dark
may the rama claim
only sustenance
may
the karakia remind people
to leave the many behind
to become many more
where you live and love
where you kanikani!
E tuna mā,
āmiomio tonu
loll, lurk, live serenely
into the future
kei roto i o koutou wai.

Don't You Ever Lie!

Tahui (Polly) Crawford

I wonder how many children have felt like me at school? My earliest memory is Form One at Te Karaka. I didn't understand the work, and I guess because I didn't show much interest in the work, the teachers didn't show much interest in me either!

My Mum told all of us that we were not allowed to leave school until we were 18. I was only 12 at the time, and I couldn't help but think—Am I ever going to learn anything?

I was seventeen and had just finished my second year in Form Five —no achievements except in Sports. My parents were worried, and I heard my Mum say to Dad—Tom, she will have to go back, and this will be her Third year in the Fifth form? What should we do?

They sent me to the Mormon College in Hamilton. I was happy because I was shy, and I thought maybe a change would be good for me.

There was this American Indian. He was the English Teacher. He was kind and took an interest in me. He saw something behind this shy student. In his class, he kept asking me questions. He knew I knew the answers—How? Because my timetable was structured so I took both of his English classes every day. He would ask me questions in the afternoon class, and I would always get the answers wrong.

That must have puzzled him, and so one day, he asked me to stay behind and asked: "Polly, when I ask you a question, you give me the wrong answer – why? You did the class this morning, so you know the answer."

I bent my head in shame and replied, "well, I wish you wouldn't ask me – I know the answer, but the rest of the class didn't do your morning class. If I answer correctly, they will think, 'she's clever,' which would be a lie, and I would feel like a cheat."

He didn't say anything, just nodded and smiled. From that day on, he never asked me a direct question; instead, he would say, "Ok, Polly, we discussed this in the morning session. Can you add anything to what we discussed this morning"—and I would.

I would always be grateful to this kind teacher who took an interest in me and my learning. In my English class the year before at Te Karaka, there were twenty-six students in my class, and I was ranked number twenty-six. The following year at the Mormon college, I was the top of the class, which helped me in my other subjects.

To be honest, it also helped to get my first job—with the Bank of New South Wales. I only had to provide them with my last year's school reports.

From the Beginning of Corona with No End

Karen Morris-Denby

We listened to the silence as it shuddered
through the treetops where dancing leaves took flight
through air we found much cleaner and believed
we gasped much easier through the darkest night

Cars sat idle in garages and driveways as people walked
and talked and waved at strangers every day
we spotted the bears dolls and toys and smiled
at kiddies who ran and jumped and giggled along the way

Lovers shrugged groaned and tumbled
as babies grew beneath the bulging breasts
of mothers who feared and trembled
when a fool spat on everyone in jest

Scientists muttered and murmured while they
played with vaccines petri dishes and scopes
the world cowered in horror wondering if

the humanity would suddenly lose all hope

Ghost and reapers drifted and creeped
along the naked streets
Where autumn leaves twirled and whirled
in pools in the midday heat

Dusty mannequins' limbs akimbo smiled like robots
with fingers pointing to a nowhere we could feel
while rainbows reflected through empty windows
of all stores as we were brought to heel

Mangey canines followed their tails in dirty doorways
where empty bowls shone in the morning sun
as rotting garbage waited for men in high viz vests
jumping from groaning trucks and ran races they never won

Empty cafes that once brimmed with lattés
and girls with silken legs beneath short skirts
showed rows of silent chairs on tables
gathering dust and dirt

In the Name of Love

Karen Morris-Denby

forgotten lovers
memories have passed through time
erased forever

shadows glide on walls
passion has no enemies
make love in all rooms

love is in the air
secret glances across crowds
hearts bruise easily

illusions of love
found in every beating heart
dreams always broken

once sealed with passion
ownership of bodies reign
unsaid law of love

eyes reflect a soul
cupid's arrow finds its mark
all love is lethal

behind drawn curtains
secret lovers play their games
guilt hangs in the air

the essence of love
hardened hearts a mystery
never to be found

secret lovers hide
under covers of darkness
lies will hold for now

cherished memories
fade as each year passes
mists of love linger

romance illusional
found in every lonely mind
canine more faithful

new-born mothers love
tender caring emotions
unconditional

roses speak of love
bouquets sent with dreamer dreams
honourable plan

passion embraces
silken lips no boundaries
lust opens all doors

hearts hardened with age
love deals many mysteries
broken promises

lovers entwined find
passion in shadowed corners
dreamers ecstasy

words of love spoken
through flickering emotions
tell beautiful lies

Quizzical Kid

Karen Morris-Denby

FADE IN:

EXT: 1950's NZ SUBURBAN BACKYARD—DAY

Sitting on the grass next to an old CHOOKHOUSE and a MOTORBIKE with a SIDECAR is TOPSY MORRIS (10) a Polynesian girl, who never smiles. She is stoic and does not like to be hugged or cuddled. She wears a tutu and a large sunhat. Topsy has many heroes she likes to emulate. Today she is Margot Fonteyn. Topsy is wearing STAGE MAKE-UP on her face. As she makes DAISY CHAINS, HAYLEY, a white chook scratches in the lawn. Topsy puts one around Hayley's neck and pouts her lips as though giving Hayley a kiss.

GRACE (VOICE OVER YELLING)
Topsyyyyy!

Topsy scoops up Hayley in her arms. Topsy Runs and does an impressive long jump.

INT: MORRIS'S HALLWAY—DAY

Topsy carries Hayley.

FRED MORRIS palagi, a tradie, late 30's cheery disposition, large but not fat, feels he has married above his station stops in front of Topsy.

FRED
I don't think so, Margot Fonteyn.

Fred grabs Hayley.

TOPSY
You're not the boss of me! You're not my real father!

GRACE MORRIS, palagi, 30's, skin like porcelain, smart casual dress, sophisticated, comes into the hall. She takes Topsy by the arm.

GRACE
We're very late.

TOPSY
You're not my real ...

GRACE
Stop that nonsense.

TOPSY
I hate...y...ballet!

INT: TOWN HALL—NIGHT

FIVE 10-year-old BALLET GIRLS dance like flaying Swan Lake cygnets. Topsy stands out with her brown face amongst the palagi girls.

INT: TOWN HALL BACKSTAGE—NIGHT

The ballet troupe are lined up for a photograph.

NEWSPAPER PHOTOGRAPHER
Smile.

A very BRIGHT FLASH
BLACK

EXT: CHOOK HOUSE—DAY

Topsy wears an oversized leather jacket, a motorbike helmet and large motorbike boots. She sits with Hayley in the chook house. Topsy reads the newspaper. Topsy sees her noticeably brown face in the photo of her ballet troupe. She is the only girl not smiling.

OFF SCREEN GRACE (YELLING)
You'll start growing feathers if you stay in there. Come and get your dinner.

Topsy spits on her finger and rubs her face from the photo. She lines the chook nest with the newspaper. While placing straw on top she finds an egg. Topsy picks up Hayley and plonks her on the egg.

EXT: OUTSIDE CHOOKHOUSE—DAY

Topsy feigns riding a motorbike.

TOPSY
Brrrrmmmm, brrmmm.

EXT: NZ SUBURBAN VILLAGE—DAY

Topsy wears an old WWI pilot helmet and swimming goggles. With her arms outstretched she is 'flying' down the street.

EXT: RETAIL BABY SHOP—DAY

Topsy stands at the window of the shop. In her hands is a battered piggy bank. Topsy suddenly appears to make a decision and rushes inside the shop.

INT: RETAIL BABY SHOP—DAY

Topsy's big brown eyes can just be seen above the counter. A matronly SHOPKEEPER peers down at Topsy.

TOPSY

Please may I see all your white babies.

SHOPKEEPER
Pardon?

TOPSY
I want to buy a baby. A brother or sister.

SHOPKEEPER
Oh?...Well... Oh?...Well...um....
SHOPKEEPER appears unfazed but is actually gobsmacked.

TOPSY
My mother. NOT my real mother, said she bought me from a baby shop.

SHOPKEEPER
Goodness. I don't sell babies.

Topsy puts her piggy bank on the counter and shakes out a pile of coins.

SHOPKEEPER
You have saved a lot. But, I'm sorry. I don't have babies.

TOPSY
When will you get some?

SHOPKEEPER
I have a lovely doll who wets her nappies.

Shopkeeper takes a pretty doll from the shelf.

Topsy scoops the coins from the counter and returns them to the piggy bank. The Shopkeeper helps her.

TOPSY

No thank you.

Topsy puts her arms out and 'flies' out of the shop.

INT: TOPSY'S BEDROOM—TWILIGHT

Topsy fashions a wig from the long blonde hair from her dolls. She is sticking the hair onto a sunhat. WHITE POWDER is on Topsy's face. Posters of HAYLEY MILLS and DEBBIE REYNOLDS are on the wall. Newspaper items and postcards of EDMUND HILARY, YVETTE WILLIAMS, BERT MUNRO and BRUCE MCLAREN also line the walls. A heap of bald dolls is piled in the corner of the bedroom. Topsy puts on the sunhat that she had stuck on long bits of blonde doll's hair.

Fred pokes his head around the door.

FRED

You going to listen to 'It's money or the bag?'

Topsy puts on adult size dark sunglasses.

INT: MORRIS'S SITTING ROOM—TWILIGHT

Fred and Topsy are seated near a large tube radio. Selwyn Toogood is asking questions.

SELWYN (VOICE OVER)
Yvette Williams won a gold medal for what athletic event?

CONTESTANT
Long jump.

SELWYN (VOICE OVER)
Correct. What is the capital of Norway?

ANON (VOICE OVER)
Oslo.

Background clapping.

SELWYN (VOICE OVER)
Where was the destination of the first long distance flight from New Zealand?

TOPSY
Antarctica! Antarctica!

ANON (VOICE OVER)
London?

SELWYN (VOICE OVER)
Antarctica.

The sound of the quiz continues in the background.

FRED

Good on you Topsy. How did you know?

TOPSY

I just know.

GRACE enters the room. She carries mugs of milo.

GRACE

Take that ridiculous thing off your head.
Is that my powder? Wash it off. Now.

Topsy gives Grace the evil eye

TOPSY

My real mother wouldn't be crabby like you.

EXT: MORRIS'S CHOOKHOUSE—TWILIGHT

TOPSY sits in the chook house. Hayley sits on the nest. Streaks of Light come through the chook house matching the tear-streaked lines through the powder on Topsy's face. The chook house door opens. Fred's arm appears around the door with a TT2 ice block in his hand. Fred squeezes in and concertinas himself beside Topsy. Fred offers the TT2. Topsy looks at the ice block but doesn't take it.

FRED

Hey girlie...

Topsy is sulking. Fred begins singing.

FRED

Beautiful beautiful brown eyes,
beautiful beautiful brown eyes,
beautiful beautiful brown eyes,
I'll never love blue eyes again ...

Topsy takes the TT2 and slowly unwraps the packet.

FRED continues singing

You are our sunshine our only sunshine

Fred and Grace love you every day
we think you're wonderful and very
clever we want to help you in every way

Topsy leans on Fred and he picks up Hayley and puts her on Topsy's knees.

GRACE (YELLING VOICE OVER)

Unless you two are laying eggs, come inside for tea.

EXT: SUBURBIA—Day

A motorbike and sidecar sedately cruise the streets. Fred is driving with Topsy in the sidecar. They pull up outside the city hall. A large banner is across the City Hall entranceway. 'QUIZ KIDS ANNUAL CHAMPIONSHIPS'

INT: CITY HALL—DAY

Topsy is on stage with 3 other YOUNG PEOPLE. They are seated at a long table with buzzers in front of them and microphones. A headmasterish QUIZZ MASTER holds a pile of quiz cards. A large banner ' QUIZZ KIDS NATIONAL CHAMPIONSHIPS' is across the stage. Score cards are placed in front of each competitor. They all have 7 points.

QUIZZ-MASTER
What is the highest mountain in New Zealand?

Topsy's buzzer lights up.

QUIZZ-MASTER
Topsy Morris?

TOPSY
Mount Cook.

QUIZZ-MASTER
Correct.

A WOMAN of small stature replaces Topsy's card with the number 8.

QUIZZ-MASTER
What is Edmund Hilary famous for? Topsy Morris.

TOPSY
The first man to climb to the top of Mount Everest

QUIZZ-MASTER
Correct.

The WOMAN replaces Topsy's card with the number 9.

QUIZZ-MASTER
Who is the first New Zealand female Olympic gold medal winner?

TOPSY
Yvette Williams.

QUIZZ-MASTER
Correct. Topsy Morris. I would like to pronounce you the New Zealand's junior champion quizz Kid of the year.

AUDIENCE APPLAUSE erupts. Fred is beaming in the audience and clapping madly.

INT: TOPSY'S BEDROOM—DAY

Topsy wears a dress. The back zip is undone. She is holding a wee CHICK. Hayley is in a cage on the dresser. Topsy is looking at her wall of fame. A Newspaper photo of Topsy with her Kids Quizz Champion certificate and cup is on the wall. The actual certificate is leaning against the cup under the photograph. GRACE enters wearing a MATERNITY SMOCK. GRACE stands next to Topsy and looks at the photograph.

GRACE

Well done Topsy.

GRACE zips up Topsy's dress.

GRACE

Who are we today?

Topsy picks up the certificate and points to her own name. Topsy grins. Hayley clucks.

FADE

Fifteen Metre Play Table

Russia in February

Benita H. Kape

Only two men; one at each end
of a very long white table, said
to be fifteen metres.

A low arrangement of flowers
at the centre. Photoshop has swept
the flowers aside and replaced

with a couple of skaters; another
gives us a delicate rendition
of the Madhatter along with Alice.
No one expects a floweriness of words;

especially from the little man
on the left. He is said to be
spoiling for war.

A clumped and ornate column
of short pillars, three of them,
hold the table to the required height.

A disproportionate scene.
The comedy of the day?

And more's the improbabilities
as Italian companies, *and* then
the Spanish make claims

as to who manufactured
a fifteen metre table. These
were no comedies. Now

the man who chose such

a metaphor for 'his' world,
sits there despised and alone.

In a Negotiated Past

A Gift of Helmets

Benita H. Kape

In a negotiating past
Minsk 11.

At the time of its signing
Angela Merkel spoke
for Germany.

The days went by and
Olaf Scholtz took his turn
at the improbable table
in Russia.

Having sat at the fireside
with Biden in Washington.
Intervening; table upon table

with Macron and Zslensky.
Olaf Scholtz reminds the world

Germany sends no weapons

to the Ukraine; support in the way
of helmets; 5000! Should
Scholtz have kept one aside

to wear at the table in Moscow?
Not exactly. but, he sat there;
bare headed and bald statements.

It was not Putin's country on
which to make a decree,
Luhansk and Donetsk.

Though they are part of Ukraine,
as he makes ready for war, he names
them countries in their own rights?

Swiftly Western Allies move
with sanctions. Nord Stream 2,
the gas line for which Germany

had waited and which had cost
Russia billions, is dead in the water.
Another weird speech from Putin.

Within hours the invasion had begun.
And rapidly the news changes;
reticence to rapid deployment.

Scholtz, the reluctant, is to forward
one thousand anti-tank weapons

plus 500 "Stinger," surface to air

missiles, to help where words failed.
Putin who was deaf to the world's
negotiations. His mind long made up.

But I do not mock a gift of helmets.
They too could save a lives.

Under the grill/ grille/grillz

Rengay (solo) sequence

Benita H. Kape

king prawns under the grill
honing a culinary skill
old as time

open air spit
a large feast under the moon

main-street grating
using a wire coat-hanger
to retrieve my glasses

a court of crows
grille to the death
one gone rogue

turning the heat down

she deletes the letter 'e'

hip hop dentistry
grillz, would you believe
and you show a little gold

Yesterday's Poem

Benita H. Kape

This is the; 'Should have
been written yesterday poem;
how lucky to be written at all
poem.' It is also, the, 'I'll write
straight onto the computer poem.'

'This is the little bit grateful poem;
I'm coming alive poem: early in
the morning poem; a little bit
bleary eyed poem' – but hey 'Going
quite well poem.'

It could be, 'The I don't have to be
a very long poem.' or 'How did I get
this long poem?'

And now it becomes 'The I'm getting
hungry poem; what's for breakfast poem;
avacado and bacon on toast poem.'

'Sorry, I have to go; my mouth is full poem.'
Yesterday's poem; Haeremai.

Whispers

Lien Ruelens

He knew it was wrong. He knew that anything to do with the Blood God was something you stay thousands of miles away from. But James was hopeless, he was desperate for a resolve, a *cure*.

James' wife was sick, very sick. There was no cure in existence. All she could do was lie on her bed and slowly die. So, he started looking among things that didn't exist, the things that people called legends or ghost stories.

James entered the ancient cave. Everything in there screamed at him to run, get away. Stepping further into the cave, he saw numerous tunnels, each labelled with dried blood. A shiver ran down his spine as he cautiously inched through the tunnel labelled '*Life and Death*.' Bloodied knives and axes stuck into the walls, and a haunting aura hung thick in the air.

A weak light flickered at what James presumed was the end of the tunnel. As he drew closer, he saw a dull flame dancing in a grand, marble fireplace. He stepped into an extravagant room with delicately polished walls and floors - not what he expected in the heart of a cave system.

Huge marble pillars supported the rocky ceiling, where, a massive chandelier hung. At the back of the room stood an immense, golden throne. Upon the throne sat the looming figure of a god, the Blood God. Everything from his jet-black hair to his armoured boots and bloody axe screamed danger. Fear rooted James' feet to the floor. the thick, threatening aura almost suffocating.

"Kneel, mortal," the Blood God commanded. James sank to his knees, the cold, hard marble clawing at his kneecaps.

"Tell me what you want from me and I'll name my price." The Blood God's deep voice boomed.

James nodded, struck with fear, but he knew better than to disrespect a God. As he made his request, the Blood God muttered under his breath and rolled his eyes, obviously not bothered by James' sob story or helpless pleading.

"I have a policy here, a soul for a soul, I save your wife, you give me your soul and become my patron," the Blood God replied.

James, desperate, paused to consider. Did he want to owe his soul to the embodiment of the devil for the rest of time? He thought of how broken and frail his wife looked, lying on the bed, clinging to slowly draining life, and decided.

At his verbal agreement, the Blood God smiled, cruel and cold. He snapped his fingers and two identical necklaces appeared. A small, glass orb was attached to each of the chains, containing two drops of blood that though incredibly similar, never mixed together.

"These necklaces contain a drop of your blood and your wife's. If one of these necklaces breaks, your wife will die and our bond will be broken."

The necklaces floated toward James' outstretched hands.

"Out," the God ordered. James hurried back through the tunnel he came from, necklaces in hand.

James put on one of the necklaces. The chain dug into his neck uncomfortably. He hid it underneath his shirt not wanting to attract attention from the town folks. The guards nodded at him as he entered the enclosed town, he reached his house soon enough, hopeful for his wife's return back to health.

He entered the house quietly and rushed to the bedroom, his wife lay motionless on the bed. Her skin was pale and her hand that rested above the covers trembled slightly. The only sign she was alive was the gentle rise and fall of her chest with every breath.

Walking to her bedside he smiled down at her and gently removed the other necklace from his pocket. Sucking in a deep breath, he put the necklace around her neck, fastening the clasp at the back. Colour seeped back into her face, her hand stopped trembling and she began to wake up.

James released the breath he didn't realise he was holding and immense joy overcame him. She sat up and looked at James with the most beautiful smile in the world. "You did it," she whispered to him. James felt tears threaten to spill from his eyes. He found the cure, she was in his arms, alive and looked better than ever before!

The rest of the day was spent celebrating his wife's return to health with the town's people. He felt that nothing could dampen his mood, but he was very wrong. That night he sat on the porch stairs, his wife fast asleep, but the Blood God's haunting smile appeared every time he closed his eyes.

He heard a low husky whisper and looked around for the source. but saw nothing. He heard it again, and this time was able to understand. 'Blood' was what it said. His face paled when he realised the whisper was coming from inside his mind.

Days turned into weeks, weeks into months, months into years. Slowly the necklace corrupted him, the cry for blood too hard to resist, his killings known only to his wife, late-night confessions somehow soothing his troubled soul. She watched as the man she once knew and loved turned into a bloodthirsty monster.

The voices spurred him on, screaming at him till they were fed. His wife didn't recognize him, it was like he had traded his life for hers, maybe that was the plan all along. She couldn't bear it any longer, she couldn't live while he was in such misery.

One night he returned home, hands and clothes bloodied, he had given into the whispers again. He changed his clothes and washed away the blood, his normal routine after he fed them.

He returned to the living room to see his wife waiting for him, and she looked at him with tears in her eyes. He wondered why she was crying but he quickly saw it, her hand was closed around the chain.

"What—what are you doing?" he stammered. He reached for her hand in an attempt to stop her.

"This is my choice, James," she said, tears spilling down her face.

Her tiny hand pulled hard on the chain and flung the necklace to the ground. The orb smashed on the ground and the drops of blood stained the floor. The world seemed to turn in slow motion as he watched his wife's lifeless body fall.

He screamed in pain, sobbing and crying over her dead body. Through his grief, he didn't notice the absence of the voices. The bond was broken, and his soiled soul returned to him. He stayed there for days, the numbness of the pure pain drove all cries for water or food from his body.

A week later the town's people found the two bodies lying together on the floor, her sacrifice was in vain, for he could not live without her.

Shapes

Paddy Noble

Undulating
Moving
Brooding
Shapeshifting
Life creating
Giving birth
Pushing and pulling
Water breaking
Strewn on this earth
Shapes, curving, soft and weak
Blood and water
Covered in skin
Joining mother
and baby cord
Tears of pain
Tears of joy
Hope
And Fear
Shakes her spirit

Life awakes
Lets you in
Baby crying
beautiful face
Symmetry in full design
Lines and curves
Circles, and shapes
Soft, delegate
A miracle touch
Taller than a proud man
Wider than a mother's smile
Span of life
Breathing
Her mother
In and out
Goddess
God
The circle of life
Life and death
Symmetry of life
Tracing the line
Meeting the cross
Sliding the curve
Touching the circle
Asymmetry
Hands and feet
Black and white
Big and small
Colours abound
Patterns open
Open the door
Life comes through

That whiff of air
Letting her spirit through
A Goddess is born
Kali, fearless
brave and strong
Papatuanuku
Her bodies worth
Feet, solid stands
Upon her earth
Baby is born
girl child
Tired and quiet
Symmetry curved in ball
Beautiful girl
Rest little thing
Your mother sleeps.

Amelie

Moana Hoogland

When the clouds drop and blend into the mountains, you know you're in trouble. And when disharmony echoes throughout the sky-world in the form of dark sky music and the trees dance in time to the flashing lights, well, that's when you pack up camp quick smart. Of course, Amelie wasn't the kind of girl to pack up camp quick smart. On the contrary, she stood on the rock jutting over the tops of the pine forest, letting the pots fly away like hawks from a cage. Though saying she 'stood', in this instance, is an understatement. Amelie leant into the wind, almost horizontal to the forest beneath. Her sharp green eyes were closed in such a way to indicate she was asleep, of course she wasn't. The gusts of wind whipped up the hem of her silver-grey frock (not the best attire, by the way, for a girl gone bush) and attempted to rip it off her. The wind raised the little hairs along her legs and arms. Amelie's white blonde hair tangled and untangled behind her in confusion. Typical Amelie. The only thing that brought her out of her trance was when Jake, the border collie she found in the bush, started barking at the assorted objects flying around.

The last rope securing her blue tarp to the ground was unravelling as she leapt on it. It seemed to jump and buck under her slight weight but she lay on it and tried to fold it in half. The wet wind immediately filled it like a parachute and she even lifted a foot in the air before she let it go and it deflated. Rolling a nearby rock on the corner she squatted and had a rethink about what she was doing. Random items from her camp were rolling around or flying, and she'd have to collect those up, but where was she going to go now? She could practically see the rain collecting in the clouds above, ready to drop.

'Jake!' She had to compete with the thunder to call the dog but the old girl came running. And yes, Jake's the perfect name for an old female dog with one brown eye and one green.

'Good girl, we gotta pack up now or we'll die of hypothermia. Let's go.' Amelie reached out and caught her canvas bag as it whizzed by on the ground. Where the tarp used to be was a weird rock hollow where the pair had slept for almost a week. Her torn and stinky sleeping bag curled in on itself and she picked it up and pulled the hood over her head. The bottom whacked her ankles, and half fluttered half dragged along behind as she picked up interesting random stuff that had run away with the storm. The tiny pot and pan, a box of matches, comb, book on surviving the wilderness, drink bottle, and the last of her salt. Her jacket was gone with the wind but she could live with that. Salt was pretty important, at least, she thought. She read somewhere that people need salt. And citrus, but there were no lemons around. She'd already run out of baked beans and 2-minute noodles. Soon she'd have to deal with the bush, maybe even eat possums. Yech!

'One day, Army' she said to herself, using her old nickname. 'you're gonna have to grow up.'

Jake barked as if to second it, and God let loose the torrent. The deluge soaked Amelie and the dog in an instant. She quickly rolled up the tarp and tied the ropes around it. The hood of her sleeping bag muted the droning of the rain, and her back was warm from reflected body heat. She righted herself and tucked the tarp under her arm.

'C'mon Jake.' She said and went to step purposefully down the hill.

But alas, when a small twelve-year-old girl goes to step purposefully down a hill, in the middle of a thunderstorm when the ground is wet through for a couple of metres, things do not end well. Instead of stepping purposefully down the hill, Amelie latched onto that tarpaulin for dear life as her leg slipped forward from underneath her and she flipped and spun in the air before landing on a brand-new mud slide upside down and unconscious. Just because she was unconscious didn't mean the rain let up. It just meant she wasn't able to feel herself sliding down the mountainside. Or the sticks and stones that scratched and bruised her. Nor could she hear Jake barking and racing after her. It meant she didn't know she'd reached the bottom, unable to move. And she didn't notice Jake, that beautiful dog, whining and worrying at her, and she didn't wake when Jake licked at the long deep scratch on Amelie's arm and lay down beside her through the storm.

A solitary planet hung in the land of mist. Fog reined the forest world with a heavy hand. Amelie opened her eyes a fraction, just enough to see the sun as if it were in a black and white movie. She saw the forest a few feet above ground, then all was lost as the cool grip of fog clenched the trees in its fist. No movement. She didn't feel like moving. Already knowing that if she did, she would be in a lot of pain. Her top arm seemed frozen in place; and she didn't really want to look at it in case it was blood. The cool mud hugged her cheek and was surprisingly comforting. As her senses returned, she heard the dripping of water and felt Jake's body heat in the small of her back. Amelie heard the quiet whistle of someone in the distance.

Pipi at Taruheru River

Daphne Poi Maxwell

I'm going to river today to get pipi.
I love eating pipi.
The rivers' mud becomes my second skin.
Ahh - reka nga pipi.

Here come the school kids again.
They always laugh and point at me
but I don't care.
I've had my feed of pipi
and I'm going to town now to get me some lollies.
There are so many lollies in pick n mix
but I love the mushroom ones the best.

My friends turn up again.
They usually come to take me home.
I know they're my friends because they know name
and they know where I live.

I want to get home before Nan sees I'm gone.
She was having a moe when I left.

I'll be home soon
and I won't need to ride my bike.
My friends will take me home in their flash car
and I'll be home in no time.

My belly is full and satisfied
now I've had my pipi and pick n mix.
Later I'm going to paint my bike
and the laundry door
and the bathroom walls - Kakariki!
I think nan will love that colour
and she will be so happy with me.

Mokopuna

Daphne Poi Maxwell

Mokopuna
Mokopuna tekau mā   rima
Mokopuna tekau mā   ono
Mokopuna

Haere ki o tī   puna
Haere ki o mā   tua
Haere ki a Ihowa
Haere

Mokopuna
Mokopuna tekau mā   whitu
Mokopuna tekau mā   waru
Mokopuna

Haere ki o tipuna
Haere ki o mā   tua
Haere ki a Ihowa
Haere

Mokopuna
He kōtiro? He tama?
Mokopuna

Haere ki o tī   puna
Haere ki o mā   tua
Haere ki a Ihowa
Haere

Mokopuna
Arohaina   i nga wā katoa
Mokopuna.

Mo a māua tamāhine me a rāua pēpi i materoto

Wharepaku

Daphne Poi Maxwell

When I turned 5 I had to go to school.
I didn't want to go to school.
I wanted to go to the river and eat pipi.

But Nan said I had to go to school because that's the rules.
Who makes the rules?
Nan said school will be good for me
because I'll make friends and learn a new language.

I like being at school with the other kids
but I don't understand a word the teacher is saying.
Maybe she thinks I'm deaf or dumb
because I don't answer her when she speaks to me.

But I'm not dumb—I can hear her perfectly.
She's speaking the new language
that I have to learn
but I don't understand a word she's saying!

I want to go to the wharepaku

but I don't know how to say 'wharepaku'
in her language.
Her voice gets loud.
She waves her arms in the air for me to sit down.

I wave my hands in the air and yell
Wharepaku! Wharepaku!

But now it's too late.
The kids laugh and point at me.
The teacher grabs me by my shirt
and drags me out of the room.
I don't know why she is treating me like this.
If only she let me go to the
Wharepaku.

I feel ashamed

Another school day
and it's play time.
I love play time at school.
I don't have to speak the new language at play time
but I know the word for Wharepaku now...
Toilet!

White Gum Motel

Daphne Poi Maxwell

Pulled in White Gum Motel, been on the road 8 hours now.
Greeted at the door as she stepped in.
"Are you right?!"
"We're looking for 2 rooms, do you have 2 for the night?"
"Rooms here are $155, down the street they're $88".
Arm across the door.
"Will call them if you wait".
"No $155 is fine, shower, rest a glass of wine.
Been on the road 8 hours, have some dinner then retire".
"Rooms here are $155, down the street they're $88.
More suited to your budget. I will call them if you wait!".
"As I said the price is fine, I can pay the $155".
"That's what you people say, but you don't really want to pay.
Trash the room, drink the mini bar booze, then you're gone before the next day".
Pulled out White Gum Motel, her head held high.
Your $155 is not worthy of my presence!

Tapping out

Vanessa Ngarimu

I would like to dedicate this piece I wrote for anyone going through grief of losing a loved one to suicide. I hope my story inspires other people who are finding it hard to express themselves through the grieving process to write it down.

All I know is that it's an emergency. I reluctantly exit the vehicle and stand at the end of the gravel driveway. My feet automatically fix to the earth. My roots spread rapidly like a time-lapse, feeling out the situation.

Ploughing through the whenua, my Wairua bursts up above the surface and into the surrounding trees. I can hear it; it sounds like white noise rushing ahead at third eye level.

My vision is clouded, I see nothing but blurry colours.

My heart is racing and yet it wants to stop.

I can't breathe.

I wait in agonising anticipation for the feedback from my Wairua.

I start to shake.

Something's wrong, I can feel it in my bones.

My wairua knows

A sense of dread comes over me.

I'm scared of what I am about to encounter.

I take a deep breath. My senses regather. Things become a little clearer.

An ambulance is backed up and staring me in the face. Not a good sign.

I can't see him, but I hear my uncle's voice. Counting aloud in rhythmic beats. He's tired but I can hear his determination.

I know what he is doing but I still don't want to look.

A medic spots me. Trying to avoid eye contact, I accidentally catch her glance. She gestures at me to go closer.

I advance forward and around the back of the ambulance door.

There's my big sister, crying like our grandmother used to. Looking down I spy my brothers' legs. Limp. Only moving from the momentum of the CPR that my uncle is performing on him. I don't want to look any further.

"WHAT THE FUUUUUUCK???"

My head and heart are racing.

I'm screaming, but nothing is coming out.

Sweat is building and I feel sick.

Survival mode kicks in.

There are other people there. I can feel their presence, but I can't see them.

I look at my sister. I send her a telepathic message that only siblings can decipher. Confirming that she receives it, she looks at me. Her eyes angle upward toward the ceiling, and she forces them shut tight.

Instinctively, I already know what's up there.

I take a deep breath and inhale the familiar scent of chainsaw oil mixed with empty beer bottles and marijuana. A subtle hint of aftershave hovers about. That's my uncle. For some strange reason, his scent gives me hope and strength to look up.

A frayed rope dangles from a beam. Whoever had to cut it, struggled. Immediately my worry turns to rage. I am angry but I don't know why.

I finally find the strength to look at him. My little brother, lying on his garage floor.

Lifeless. Pale. His complexion is wrong.

I feel my heart shatter into a million pieces. It hurts so bad.

This is all new to me and I fucking hate it.

I can't even help him.

I watch my uncle's sweat dripping from his forehead onto his beloved nephew's chest. A medic asks him if she should take over.

He refuses.

Thoughts race through my head.

"I only saw you last night. We talked and we laughed. We moved furniture between mine, yours, and nans. What happened between then and now? You seemed ok but I didn't know you weren't. You couldn't wait to kick back on your hand-me-down couch and write some new lyrics. Why didn't you tell me?"

I realise I am angry at myself. For not being here, for not risking one more time in the dogbox just to hang out with him. That sacrifice could have been the difference.

I try to speak to him in the same telepathic sibling energy I did with our sister.

"Wake up. Please just wake up. It's ok, please don't leave us".

It's not working. He's not picking up. He's out of service. His battery is flat.

I now must try to connect another way. I dig deep and yell from the pit of my stomach. I not only want him to hear me, but I also want our tīpuna and all the gods to hear me too.

"YOU FUCKING GET UP RIGHT NOW!!"

I scream it over and over. It still isn't working.

No one is listening to me.

I start to panic.

I want to punch him.

I want to punch anybody.

My self-control is slipping away, and I can't pull it back in. I fall to the ground and dig my hands into the dirt. My roots aren't spreading out this time. My Wairua is confused and hides itself in our shell. We're not even a metre away from each other, but we aren't connecting. His aura is dull. I look frantically for a sign. Not a bird, not an animal, not a breeze...nothing.

"Fuck this! Fuck you! This isn't real! Fuck the world!!"

For the first time in my life, I am helpless, I am speechless, I am confused, I am truly lost. I feel so disconnected, from everything. I am weak and I am vulnerable. I feel stripped, I feel ripped off. I am just a shell, even my wairua needed time out and deserted me.

It hasn't been confirmed, but I sense that this is it.

He is tapping out.

My submission is the story of a part of my grief that I tried to block out. The more I tried to forget about it, the more it ate me up. So, I decided to face and acknowledge it, I just didn't know how, until the Year 7-8 class I was helping, did a session on descriptive writing. This is the first time in 6 years I have felt some relief.

Haere Haere Haere Atu Ra

Taranga Kent

The clouds gather
Rolling in over these long familiar hills
Sombre and cimmerian as our tangi garb
Coming to pay their respects
Like the rest of us

It's the wailing that gets me every time
The embodiment of insurmountable pain
Piercing me to the core
Liquifying my bones
Powerless and impotent in the face of death

Kawakawa halos
crown our kuia
as they call to those long gone
Fronds in gnarled hands swaying
to the rhythm of love and loss

So much to laugh about
So much to cry about
The waiata slip off my tongue
Blending with a hundred other mournful voices
Raised in grief and celebration

Tears flow freely
From the people
And from the sky
Ranginui's mingling with mine
Soothing, caressing

Lid on, turning of screws
Shutting out light and life
E kui, we surrender you
to the deep, dark embrace
of Hine-nui-te-po

Homeless

Taranga Kent

Bedding down for the night
In doorways, below bridges
A cardboard mattress the only barrier
from the freezing ground
Gloved hands gripping
A paper bag full of warmth
Stories to tell
But no-one to listen
Unloved
Unwanted
Unwashed
Up at first light
Trolley full of treasures
Wheeling my way to oblivion

Ata Whakarongo

Taranga Kent

He aha te reo o te taiao?
Ko te whio o nga hau e wha
Ko te pao tawhiti o te whaitiri
Ko te karakia timatanga o te tame heihei
Ko te huihuinga reo o nga manu i te putanga o te ra
Ko nga korokoro o te tui
Ko te koakoa o te ruru i te po
Ko te karanga o te kihikihi i te raumati
Ko te ngatete o te ahi i te hotoke
Ko te waiata o te ngutu awa e rere ana ki te moana
Ko te moteatea o nga rakau i te ngahere
Ko te oriori o nga ngaru i takahuri ki te takutai
Ko enei nga reo maha o te taiao

What is the voice of the natural world?
It is the whistling of the four winds
It is the distant crash of thunder
It is the opening prayer of the rooster in the morning
It is the dawn chorus of the birds
It is the call of the cicada in summer

It is the crackle of the fire in winter
It is the song of the river as it flows to the ocean
It is the chant of the trees in the forest
It is the lullaby of the waves rolling in to the shore
These are the many voices of the natural world

A Piece of Me

Taranga Kent

I found a piece of me today
Washed up on the beach
Edges worn smooth
From tossing and turning
Between Tangaroa's sheets
Once broken and jagged
Now sanded and smooth
Like the pieces of my shattered heart
Will eventually be
In time

Nana and I

Suzanne Pinfold

"Lulla, lulla, lulla, lulla bye bye, do you want the moon to play with or the stars to run away with, they'll come if you don't cry," crooned my Nana as I lay snuggled on her lap.

My favourite place was sitting on Nana's knee, wrapped in her arms, head upon her breast, listening to her warm, soft voice singing her songs and weaving her stories. I would float and drift, caressed and cocooned in their silken magic.

As the words of the song wove themselves around me, My childhood imagination wondered how it would feel to hold a twinkling star in my hand, to run and dance with them, to throw them like balls in the air, to sprinkle stardust in my hair or to fly back home with them into the vast night sky. Magic indeed.

As I listened to her stories, I journeyed back in time to the "Olden Days", as I called them, to the time when she was a girl and life was very different. Nana wasn't allowed to run around bare-legged like me, doing flips and handstands. Instead, she said, she wore long dresses as all ladies did then, for society deemed it shocking to show your legs. That would not do at all. With a twinkle in her eye, she told me that when she was a young woman, she entered a contest for the best ankles—and won. Each time I heard that I would smile to myself and feel secretly pleased by her daring. Looking back now, I believe that underneath her uprightness, she hid a rebel soul.

Still, life in those days wasn't always prim and proper. Poor Nana was the youngest of eight children with seven older brothers who, she said, would tease her mercilessly—often chasing her around the garden with spiders on the end of sticks. I shivered whenever I heard that story, but Nana would squeeze me tighter, and tell me she wasn't too frightened and usually managed to get away. I was glad it wasn't me. Being so terrified of spiders, I would have screamed and screamed. It made me wonder if perhaps, that was just the way of brothers, as mine teased me too. I felt lucky I only had one.

Being a girl, Nana was the one who helped her mother with all the household chores: cooking, cleaning, washing and scrubbing. One day, just as she was throwing the vegetable peelings out onto the garden, her father unexpectedly came around the corner and into his big bushy ginger beard they went. I loved that story and would ask her to tell it over and over again as I could just see the shock on his face and could imagine all the peelings sticking out of his beard and the dirty water running down his face. Just the thought of it made me giggle and laugh. Although, if I remember correctly, Nana said he didn't find it at all funny.

This man, my great grandfather, drove a team of bullocks and was away from his family for months at a time hauling logged kauri trees out of the bushland. And as Nana told it, whenever he arrived back home, the first thing he did was march straight into the house and without taking off his muddy boots or even a hello, pick up my great grandmother, throw her over his shoulder and say, "Now up those stairs with you, Annie." Now I know why there were so many children.

From Nana's stories, I got the impression that Annie, although short and tiny (easy to sling over a shoulder) was a steely soul and didn't put up with anyone's silly nonsense. Even on the eve of Nana's wedding, when she nervously asked her mother what to expect on her wedding night, was told, "You just keep on scrubbing those floors girl." A no-nonsense woman, to be sure. Still, to survive in those pioneering times, often alone, with a large family to care for, and without the amenities of today, I guess you needed to be made of steely stuff.

Yet, this great grandmother of mine, must have had a softer side, and the stories of her I most loved to hear about, were those about her reading tea leaves and ordinary playing cards to help others. These tales of her lit me up with their seeming magical wonder, for I was always a child who believed in the impossible. As Nana told it, Annie even stopped my great grandfather from taking a train trip because she foresaw an accident happening that day in the dregs of his breakfast teacup. After many heated words, he eventually decided to delay his journey, which was fortunate, as once again my great grandmother's predictions were proved to be correct. Though exactly what happened to the train that day, I never thought to ask.

Nana didn't like remembering that side of her mother as she felt it was not a good Christian way to live. Nevertheless, they were my favourite stories and I was fascinated by them. Perhaps, because somewhere inside, they helped me come to terms with the things I also felt, saw and knew that others didn't. I wasn't to know it then, but I was much more like my great grandmother than I could ever have dreamt and would find myself eventually walking in her footsteps.

Although I loved my Nana's songs and stories, I loved her beautiful self most of all. Over the years, the memory of her still shines as brightly as all the stars in the sky—her soft wavy silver hair, her twinkling blue eyes, her grace and kindness. The way her hands danced and the needles clicked as she knitted and crocheted her beautiful creations. The easy times we spent in the garden together, digging, planting and harvesting. The way she would listen to me and never make fun of my so-called imaginings. I admired how she always dressed well and took good care of herself. She was a proud, beautiful, independent woman, and I am so grateful that some of her stardust rubbed off onto me.

We only had eleven years together, but through all that time she was my own personal bright shiny star, full of light and love. She always made me smile and would call me her little ray of sunshine, so perhaps we shone for each other. I hope so!

"I hope you know Nana, that you turned each song, story and every moment we spent together into starlight, which I carefully tucked away safely under the blanket of my heart. I had no way of knowing then, as I lay comfortably in your lap, how precious these stars would become."

For well into the future, when there was no light to be seen and the dark night seemingly had no end, I would take these sparkling memories out and remember. I would remember the love we shared and feel the happiness and joy of my childhood once again. I would hear your stories and draw strength from them and from all those who had gone before me. The night then, miraculously, wouldn't feel so cold and I would take courage in knowing that the golden light of the star of hope would always be there, lighting my way, no matter what may lay before me.

Motives For Murder

Dorothy M. Fletcher

Motives For Murder was originally part of the first novel in the *Abandoned Wives' and Widows' Club* series, *(Cupboards Full of Skeletons, The Girls on the Ghan* and *Life after Death.)* During one of the many rewrites and edits that most novels go through, Dorothy decided to rewrite this part of the book into a short story which would act as a free reader magnet to encourage readers to try the series. This short story gives readers a glimpse of Lydia's life before she met the group of ladies who call themselves the Abandoned Wives' and Widows' Club, and why she considered murder as an option. But did she act on her impulse?

The house reeked of silence. It had descended as a thick and tangible shroud as the last of Jack's relatives left. At the end of five long days of pretence, I could at last discard the mask of grieving widow and allow myself to admit to my real feelings—relief. After forty-two years of marriage my husband had shown the good grace to finally shuffle off and leave— permanently.

"Nan? You there?"

"Yes. In the conservatory."

Sophie's face appeared round the door. My granddaughter, the joy of my life, and the only decent adult in the family.

"Thought I better pop back and check you're coping. It's been a long day."

"Mmm," I agreed. "Grab a coffee and some left-overs and come and join me."

She disappeared for a couple of minutes and then returned with a steaming mug and a plate heaped with asparagus rolls, several vol-au-vents and a lamington.

I laughed. "Good girl. I need someone to help me wade through all that food." Sophie could always eat heaps and never lose her svelte figure. Life isn't fair—I only had to pass by a cream cake and I'd gained a kilo. "Where's Tommy?" I asked, longing to get my hands on Sophie's lovely three-year-old son.

"Em's babysitting for me. Did I tell you? She taking him to the pool and starting to teach him to swim. He loves the water."

"You're so lucky to have a flat-mate like Emma." I paused. "What did you think of the service this morning?"

Sophie was about to bite into a salmon vol-au-vent but she stopped and put it back on her plate. She sat silently for a few seconds twirling a piece of her long, blond hair and biting her bottom lip.

"It's okay," I prompted. "You can tell me what you really think."

"Well, all those things people said ... it wasn't Granddad, was it? I mean—they made him sound so nice. They called him honourable, generous, and I ask you, patient! When was the last time he was ever patient? He was a grumpy old sod. The only good bit of the service was when Jeremy—you know the young bloke he met fishing?" I nodded and smiled because I knew what was coming. "He was trying to be polite telling his bit about Granddad, and you could see he was having to choose his words carefully. When his young kid got loose and wanted his dad's attention, he ran up to his dad and started thumping him and I had a hard time not laughing. The kid's hand only reached his dad's groin. He thumped and thumped with all his might. His dad tried hard to ignore it but you could see his eyes watering in pain. The whole congregation was tittering and—"

The conservatory door flew open. "Sophie!" My daughter and Sophie's mum, Josephine, had never learnt to knock. "How can you be so disrespectful to your grandfather? We only put him in his grave three hours ago. Show a little more consideration for your grandmother's feelings." Exhausted with this outburst she flopped her rather well-padded frame into one of the bamboo chairs. "He was a saint to put up with such an unappreciative family."

Yet again I needed to defend my granddaughter. "Actually, Jo, I asked Sophie to be honest with me. Although Jack was a good father to you, he wasn't exactly grandpa of the year for Sophie, and the story she was telling was very funny. I laughed quietly myself at the time."

Josephine sat up straight, pushing her sharp nose into the air. "And whose fault was it he was never kind to her? She never liked him. She didn't even try."

Sophie put her plate on the coffee table and hung her head. I wanted to rush over and hug her but knew from experience that was the fastest way to make Jo worse. Why are some family members just put on this earth to try your patience?

"Jo," I said in the most soothing voice I could manage, "we've been through this too many times before. Adults should show the younger generation how to behave. He didn't show Sophie any love from the day she was born. Is it surprising she didn't shower him with affection?—although I know she tried. Despite what was said this morning, your father was, at times, a very difficult man to get on with." Jo started to bluster. "No. Stop that now. We need each other at the moment, so let's forget all this and work together."

"You mean you and Sophie. You always leave me out."

My patience was wearing thin. "We do not, Jo. Sometimes you won't come to see me for ages and your phone calls are very short. When I need to make decisions it's good to have someone to talk it over with and Sophie will listen to me. There will be times I'll need you, Jo. Can I count on you?"

"When was I ever able to count on you, Mum? Dad said you were always belittling me and making fun of my rescuing animals."

I had to take some deep breaths and count to ten before I could trust myself to answer. Jack had so much to answer for. "I never at any time made fun of your passion for rescuing animals. The only comment I ever made was that I thought you might enjoy keeping one as a pet rather than giving them all up for adoption."

Josephine stood up. "Anyway, I won't stop to listen to you two denigrating Dad now he's gone. I came to remind you to call if you need anything."

She turned and back went out through the conservatory.

Sophie looked at her watch. "Heavens, is that the time. I told Em I'd be back by five and I've still got to go to the supermarket to pick up some things for tea."

"Please take some of the left-overs with you. I'm sure it won't hurt Tommy to have finger-food for once."

"Are you sure?"

"I'm never going to get through it all. Most is destined for the rubbish bin, so help save the planet and eat some of it."

"Thanks, Nan."

She disappeared into the kitchen for a couple of minutes then came back with a bulging carrier full of greaseproof paper wrapped parcels. "I didn't realise there's so much left, so I've grabbed some for Emma – hope that's okay?"

"Fine. I bet I could probably still feed the five thousand."

She bent over and kissed my cheek. "You stay there, I'll let myself out. I've got to work tomorrow but I'll pop over in the evening to make sure you're okay. I wish you'd get a mobile then I could text as well." I was about to repeat all my usual excuses for not entering the technological age when she waved her hand. "See you, Nan. Love you." She blew a kiss and was gone, the front door slamming as she left the house.

When did she start looking after me? Wasn't it supposed to be the other way round? Despite a mum who had trouble showing any tender emotions and a grandfather that grew to ignore her completely, Sophie had grown into a very caring and independent woman.

I remembered the day she was born.

Jo was having problems with the whole business of giving birth. She liked things to be orderly and for her to be in control. Child birth doesn't allow for that. The body takes over, and if you fight against it, as Jo was doing, it just makes you suffer more. It didn't matter what the hospital staff did to try to get Jo to relax, she tensed up and screamed with every contraction. She wouldn't let me hold her hand or comfort her, and when I tried to put a flannel on her forehead, she grabbed it and threw it across the room. Unfortunately, Jack chose this moment to walk through the door—he got it full in the face. I tried very hard not to laugh.

"Urgh!" he spat out as he threw the flannel at me. "Get rid of that," and he stalked over to Jo.

"Daddy. Thank goodness you've come." she tried to embrace him but he pulled away, standing out of her reach. "Make this go away. I can't stand the pain any longer."

"Your fault, my girl. Told you that man was no good and this is what you get for your fornication—bringing a bastard into the world.

Pity he didn't have his accident before he'd knocked you up. Well don't expect me to have anything to do with it. We'll sort out what we're going to do when you'd had it. Until then, I'm going fishing. Goodbye." And he left.

Jo screamed—partly because her body was wracked with another urge to push, and partly because the father that she had adored all her life, had left her to cope with just me as her ally.

I think that was probably the first time the notion of killing him, seriously crossed my mind. How difficult would it be?

How different would life have been if I'd followed up on that thought? Useless to speculate. I couldn't alter history so I would just have to get on with the present. I was about to spend the night alone in the house for the first time since Jack's death. How was I going to cope on my own?

When I first met him, he appeared handsome and sophisticated, a man who knew what he wanted, and that was me. After we married, he soon degenerated into the grumpy old sod Sophie had described. When he was with Josephine, though, he was different. He was gentler with her and indulged her every whim. He mostly showed his more affable side to the world, too, which is probably why all those people had given him a glowing send off this morning. Unfortunately, to Sophie and me he was dominating, controlling and demanding, with neither of us able to come up to his expectations. He had more or less cut himself off from Sophie a few years ago. When she was first born, he tried to get Jo to sign adoption papers. I managed to persuade her not to and he reluctantly accepted that he was saddled with her. I was surprised he hadn't jettisoned me a long while back. Instead, he connived, cajoled and openly threatened me into staying in a marriage where it was obvious that neither party loved the other. Why?

Was it my fault? If only I'd tried harder to love him, would that have made things different for Josephine? For Sophie? For me?

No.

I'd known quite soon into the marriage, even before Jo was born, that he didn't love me. I was just a possession to be kept caged for reasons that I couldn't discern, and, despite searching, had never found out why he did it. These feelings of guilt rolled around my head for most of the night until eventually, at around 5 am, I must have drifted into an uneasy sleep, with visions of some evil thing threatening Sophie as a recurring theme of my dreams.

Children shouting on their way to school woke me. Although I'd only managed just over three hours sleep, I was awake, so I started another day. While I was getting breakfast, I had to remind myself to make only enough for one. Forty-two years of feeding someone else was etched in my brain and I needed to consciously think about amounts.

As the toast was browning my mind ranged back to other breakfasts in this kitchen. Me doing everything, Jack sitting in his chair with the morning paper, demanding everything. Unfortunately, nothing I could do was right. The toast was too brown or not brown enough, the porridge was never the correct consistency. When I suggested he should make it himself he would get angry, occasionally throwing things to make a point. I got very good at ducking.

Why did I stay with him? When my parents were alive I had very good reasons to stay. When they died – it was just too much effort to leave. Plus, he would have made sure I never saw Josephine again. Jo and I didn't have a good relationship, but I always had hopes that I could change that.

As I sipped my second cup of coffee, finding it strange to be the first person to read the paper, the phone rang.

"Lydia?" asked the disembodied voice on the other end.

"Yes," I replied equally succinctly.

"Peter Bellamy here," the family solicitor. "We need to do the will bit pretty soon. Are you available any time today?"

'I've nothing booked so far. What time would you like to meet?"

"How about 11.30?"

"Shall I bring Jo and Sophie with me?"

There was a pause. "No. Come on your own to begin with then we'll work out where to go from there."

I agreed and we said our goodbyes.

Strange. There again, Jack was strange. I knew he had left a will because he often referred to it and laughed, but I had no idea what was in it.

He'd probably left me nothing.

The smell of Peter's office hit me as I walked through the door —furniture polish mixed with leather and the musty smell of old books. Two walls were taken up in floor to ceiling shelving packed with leather bound books, the spines fading with age. They looked down on the occupants of the office with disdain—their position secured by the judgements held within the hide bound covers. I wondered whether he ever consulted any of them or if they were only there to uphold his position, threatening his clients with his superior knowledge. Behind his desk sat a smaller set of shelves with newer editions, even some paperbacks. Maybe these were the tomes he actually consulted.

"Lydia. Please take a seat," Peter said as he shook my hand and got me settled into his office.

"Firstly, my deepest condolences on Jack's passing. You must be finding things very difficult at the moment."

"Yes." At least that was truthful. Jack's dying had made life difficult, but not always in the ways other people imagined it. "There appears to be so much to do, so many people wanting the paperwork. Thank you for your lovely card and for speaking at the funeral. I was very touched."

He smiled. "Least I could do. I've known you both for so long. Don't worry too much about the paperwork—I can deal with most of that. Once we get the death certificate I'll get going, and hopefully things won't take too long. Now," and he picked up some papers, "the will. Do you know what's in here?" I shook my head. There was an awkward silence.

"You may be wondering why I asked you to come here without Josephine and Sophie." I nodded, not wanting to make this easier for him. My anger had made me feel as though he was in collusion with Jack. Silly really—he was only doing his job. But he was one of the people who had spoken so highly of my lately departed and unlamented husband.

"Jack left instructions that you were to come first, alone, and then I was to instruct the others. He gave me a letter to give to you."

Peter took out an envelope from amongst his papers, and instead of offering it to me he bent over to the intercom on his desk and asked his secretary to come in. She was a good-looking woman of around fifty, with a very athletic figure. She kept her head down and wouldn't meet my eyes.

"You will need to sign for it, and Sarah will witness that I have indeed handed the letter over. Routine procedure, you understand." I nodded again.

The letter was handed over and the paperwork completed. "If you could read it now, then we can look at Jack's will."

My stomach lurched and I took a few deep breaths to get my emotions under control. I had no intention of crying in the solicitor's office just because I had written confirmation of what I'd always known – that he would try to leave me penniless and destitute.

His familiar, but not the least comforting, handwriting covered the page. I looked up at Peter to find him staring intently at me. "Do you know what's in this?" I asked.

"No. Jack came in the day he died to make some alterations to his will. He gave me this and asked that you read it first and then I was to destroy it."

I read.

Lydia

If you are reading this, I am dead and buried and you have what you have always wanted from me—to be free. You've served your purpose and I'm in a place where I don't care anymore.

As you've probably guessed I wanted to leave everything to Josephine but Peter informs me that the Family Protection Act will ensure that you can contest the Will. I realise that would mean Jo would have to wait a long time to get anything so I relented, not for your sake you understand, but for hers.

I've left you the house to live in until such time as you no longer require it, then it has to go to Jo. Burn the books. You were never interested in them so I'm sure you won't miss them.

You get an amount equivalent to the superannuation to last until you reach sixty-five then it will cease. The remainder of my money will go to Jo and you can make your way in the world as best you may—I don't care. Sophie and her bastard get nothing.

Jack

My eyes were dry as I said, "Okay, Peter, you can read Jack's will now."

The nights were following the same pattern. Once I got to sleep the nightmares of Jack's return kept haunting me. This night was no different. At 2.34 am, I got out of bed and changed my sodden nightie for a dry one. By the time I'd done this I knew I was wide awake so there was no point in going back to bed. Tea – that's what I needed. I grabbed a thick dressing gown and made my way into the kitchen. Camomile – a mug of that usually calmed me down enough to sleep. I filled the jug, popped a tea bag in a mug and opened the fridge door from habit not hunger. Urgh! There was still so much food left, none of it looked or smelled appetising any longer. The sparrows would get a bonanza in the morning.

As I waited for the jug to boil, I filled in the time tidying things that had accumulated on the benches. A couple of letters lay unopened. They were both addressed to Jack. I couldn't face opening them yet. His reaction the first time I'd opened a letter was enough to put me off for life.

Jo was a few months old and I tried to love her, I certainly cared for her, but I got no emotional response back from her.

I was penned up in the house all day and I was bored.

The letter came in the morning post. It was addressed to Mr and Mrs Jack Thompson. The envelope was high quality paper and had an embossed watermark of a coat of arms. It looked exciting. I knew never to open mail addressed to Jack but this had my name on too, and he wouldn't be home for hours. I decided to hedge my bets and try to open it so it could be sealed up again.

I filled the jug from the hot water tap and put it on to boil. Soon steam was gushing out. Being careful to keep my fingers out of the way I put the seal in the steam. Gradually, very slowly, very carefully I eased the flap up until the envelope was open. I pulled the missive out and read it. It was an invitation to the annual dinner dance of the local chapter of the Society of Accountants. I'd gone to the odd one of these with Dad and they were good fun.

I folded the invitation and slid it back into the envelope. The trouble was when I tried to make the flap stick back down it wouldn't.

The glue had gone. What now? Sticky tape wouldn't do. An invitation as posh as this would not come with sticky tape holding it sealed.

There was nothing for it—I would just have to brazen it out.

I spent the spare time between looking after Jo, going through my things trying to find something to wear. There wasn't anything. I would need a new dress. Jack wouldn't like that. He didn't like being forced to buy me new clothes. After all, I only went out to the supermarket —why did I need new clothes for that?

By the time he came home I was so nervous. He stepped into the kitchen and I grabbed the envelope and pasted on a big smile.

"Look what came today. An invitation to the accountants' dinner dance. Isn't that wonderful. I haven't been out since ... I can't remember the last time. You'll get to wear your good suit and I will need a new dress. I'm sure Mum will be happy to come and babysit and ..."

He was standing absolutely still. His face was drained of colour and set into an aspect so severe I was suddenly very afraid of what he would do next. Was I safe? Was Josephine safe?

He started very quietly but with so much menace my insides were flooded with adrenaline. Fight or flight? I didn't know which.

"How dare you open mail addressed to me!" I was going to point out my name was on it too but he didn't give me a chance. "You will never, I repeat," his voice changed and I swear the walls vibrated, "never touch anything addressed to me! In fact, you will not open anything that comes into that letterbox. They are mine. Nothing to do with you."

He marched over to me until his nose was almost touching mine. I thought he was going to hit me. He grabbed the envelope. "You will not be going to any dinner dance. Your job is here looking after the baby, and I will not have your interfering parents coming to look after my Josephine. Do I make myself clear?"

I nodded.

He backed off. "I'm hungry. I'll have dinner on a tray in the lounge." He stalked off towards the bedrooms, and I heard him pick Josephine up and take her to the lounge.

As I dished up his dinner, I vowed I would make my visits to Mum and Dad's more regular, but during the day when he didn't know I was there.

The jug boiled and I waited a minute for it to cool slightly and then poured the water onto the tea bag. I took my cup to the lounge and sat in my favourite chair by the window.

Why didn't I leave him then? Too young, I guess. Too used to doing what Dad told me, and then Jack. I sat back and inhaled the steam from the camomile tea. The familiar pungent fragrance filled my senses and pushed the replay button in my brain—back to the final morning of Jack's sojourn on this Earth.

The sound of the doorbell had interrupted my struggles with a small portion of my latest daub—as Jack called my paintings. I'd painted over this small corner of Sophie's left hand so many times that the paint was starting to create a small mountain that didn't match the rest of the canvas. Next time I'd get my palette knife and scrape off the whole hand and start it again. There was no time now so I wrapped the end of my brush in a cloth soaked in thinners, laid it on the side table with the rest of my gear and went to answer the front door muttering, "From now on, I'll stick to landscapes."

As soon as I opened the door, I recognised the taller of the two young police constables who were looking very earnestly at me.

"You're young Keith Mellors, aren't you? Dot Mellors' son." He nodded, his face blushing at the same time. "I bet you don't remember me helping you with your reading?"

"I certainly do, Mrs Thompson. I remember it well." When did his voice acquire these deep bass tones? I remembered it as a boy's

light soprano. Looking at both the constables I was afflicted with that terrible insight of age—surely neither of these boys were old enough to wear a uniform—they should still be at school. And yet it was more years than I cared to remember since I had been a voluntary teacher aide at the nearby primary school, so it was quite within the realms of possibility that Keith had grown older.

I managed to get my brain back in focus. "What can I do for you, officers?"

The shorter, darker haired one answered. "I'm Police Constable Wrigley and you seem to know Police Constable Mellors. I'm afraid we have some bad news for you. Could we come in please?"

My brain started to scream – Sophie! Keith Mellors must have taken my arm and steered me through to the lounge because suddenly he was helping me to sit in Jack's armchair. I tried to get up as I knew how annoyed Jack would be if he came back from his errand and found me in his chair, but Keith put a hand on my shoulder and gently sat me down again.

PC Wrigley looked into my eyes. "I'm terribly sorry, Mrs Thompson, but there has been an accident." I felt sick as my heart plummeted into my stomach. "We believe your husband, Jack Thompson, was the driver of a car that went off Back Ormond Road and hit a power-pole. Unfortunately, he did not survive."

Jack—not Sophie. Thank goodness. I breathed a sigh of relief. Then it hit me. God! What had I done? Did they know? I looked into their eyes. There was nothing but sympathy. No disgust. No accusation. They couldn't know.

Keith patted my arm. "I'll make you some tea. Do you take milk and sugar?"

I forced my brain into working. "Er ... no. Can you find the camomile please, Keith? I'd much prefer that. Thank you."

The other young man was watching me earnestly. Maybe they did suspect something? Jack? Dead? I couldn't take it in.

"Are you sure it's Jack?"

"He had his driving licence on him and the car is registered in his name. I'm afraid we will need you to formally identify him as soon as you're able."

"Yes. Of course. Did he suffer?"

"No, ma'am. It looks very much as though he might have had an ... incident."

My heart lurched again. They did know. I must stay calm. "An incident? What do you mean?"

"A stroke or something, but we'll know better when ... I'm afraid there will have to be an autopsy, to confirm the cause of death."

That was too much. An autopsy. They were bound to find out. I collapsed in the chair into a weeping huddle. I vaguely sensed someone saying comforting things and patting my arm. The pungent fragrance of camomile wafted into my senses.

"Here you go, Mrs T. You've had a big shock. Drink this and you'll feel better."

He was right—I'd had a big shock. I never meant it to go this far.

I sipped the tea, trying to get myself back under control. "He'd only gone to the bookshop. He'd ordered a book and it had come in," I said more to myself than the two boys. Then I realised something was wrong. "I thought he'd been gone a long time. Did you say he was on Back Ormond Road?"

"Yes," Keith answered. "He was heading out of town, just past Grey's bush, on the straight there. No other vehicles were involved. There were no skid marks either which makes us think something had happened to him before he hit the power-pole."

What was he doing out there? The bookshop was in town. What was he up to?

The thought had crossed my mind that maybe he was giving the car a warm up. "Too much town driving tends to clog up the engine," he'd always said. "It needs a good warm up every now and then." But he'd gone to see his friend out past Whatatutu only the day before. Surely that would have cleaned the engine out. So where was he going?

Keith and the other police officer took me to the mortuary.

"Better to get it over with quickly," they'd said, and I wanted to be sure it was Jack before I spoke to Josephine and Sophie.

He looked peaceful. Definitely him. There wasn't a mark on his head – that was the only bit I could see. His face looked thinner as I guess the muscles had relaxed and been pulled down by gravity. I touched him—he was cold.

Definitely Jack.

Definitely dead.

The doors flew open and Jo barged in. "Why didn't you tell me? How could you be so cruel?" She fell on Jack's body and wailed. "Daddy! Daddy!"

Turning on me with mascara-streaked cheeks she yelled, "She killed him! She never loved him!"

Poor Keith tried to intervene, "It was an accident, ma'am. He drove ..."

"She drove him to it. That bitch made his life a misery until he drove himself into a power-pole."

I walked over to comfort her. "Josephine, dear," and I put a hand on her shoulder as she went back to hugging Jack. "You're distressed and overwrought. Come and have a coffee— that'll help calm you down."

She shook my hand off and turned her tortured face back to me. "Daddy's dead! But look at you. Calm, composed, not a hair out of place. I bet you're laughing inside."

I wasn't. I was empty, totally bereft of any feeling, working purely on automatic.

"That's your grief talking," I said. "I'll leave you alone with your father for a few minutes, then we'll have to go and tell Sophie."

"There's another bitch that'll be glad he's gone." She almost collapsed on top of Jack. "Daddy! Daddy! Why did you leave me?"

Keith steered me out of the mortuary and towards the café, leaving poor Constable Wrigley to deal with Jo. I felt very sorry for him.

Later, Keith dropped me off at Sophie's. Jo was still at the mortuary and I learned later that she practically had to be prised off his body. A doctor gave her a sedative and she was taken home to sleep it off.

Both Sophie and I were in the strange situation of grieving for a man that we had never loved. Together we remembered him, trying to think of happy times and eventually I did cry for him. He had behaved like a bastard towards us both, never-the-less he was part of our small family and we mourned his passing. However, for both of us, the mourning was soon overtaken by the sense of relief that that part of our lives was over.

And for me, it was the start of the guilt and foreboding.

Had I killed him?

Find out in *Cupboards Full of Skeletons*, the first in the *Abandoned Wives and Widows Club* series. Check it out at: https://www.dorothyfletcher.co.nz/

Walking as the morning sun rises after rain

Victoria Stewart

While we were sleeping
Angels dressed branches in diamonds
Hanging jewels from the tips of leaves
And the earth heaved a sigh
Flavouring the dawn with its breath

While we were sleeping
A legion of earthworms rose up
Then retreated
As the soil creaked and folded
Ready for the new day.

While we were sleeping
A feathered chorus ushered in the night
Before heralding the dawn
Competitive chattering jubilation
An orchestra singing from different song sheets.

While we were sleeping
Anything became possible again
What we did wrong became yesterday's news
And this morning became the day
When we could make dreams come true.

Liquid amber

Victoria Stewart

It was cold last night
So you put on your prettiest dress
Just to throw it off again.
Bejewelled bedazzling:
Flame red against the brilliant blue.
You always did suit
Gold against your skin.
Is this you at your finest
In the hours before you sleep?
I love you in the green of the morning.
I love you in the shade of noon.
I love you in your evening finery.
Even at night your bare arms reach for me
And hold my attention.
Stay here. Wait. Listen.
Tomorrow we will dance together again.
Renewed but still remembering.
Your fire. Your passion.
As your mantle fell to the floor
And our feet scuffed through your petticoats.

A song, less violin

Victoria Stewart

Sometimes
In a yearning for silence
And unhearing of the heard
I unwind the strings of this violin
Looser and looser
Relaxing the melody out of tautness
Until I hear nothing
No longer tuned or attuned
Released from all that resonates
Where no swiping bow
can play as much as a memory
Of an echo.

The song Dame Vera would never sing

Victoria Stewart

We'll meet again, perhaps on a zoom call,
But for now we drink solitary gins:
Stockpiling our produce for
More sociable times.
Hard to predict when our paths will cross
As we persevere in parallel lines,
Defined by the social distance that unites us,
Arms resolutely unlinked in friendship.
Queues of masked faces keep the faith,
Exposing only shine-saddened eyes
That yearn to touch.
When we come together again
We will cling awkwardly to each other
In an agoraphobic embrace
Like inverted magnets that repel in circles
Before sticking like glue
When one turns to face the other.

This Beautiful Life

W. F. Stubbs

This beautiful life
With stars to battle over,
Longing to swim in an ocean of,
Feelings to dwell in the haven of;
Where we search without meaning
and assume learning through reflections.
Have you held enough hands to warm your heart
with integrity's shadow?
Have you felt enough grains fall loosely
through eager fingers of morning's sorrow?
This beautiful life lost in tides,
Here I swim again returning thoughts to horizons
Where ships spread their sails like birds on the wind,
Breezes for salt spray and crustaceans,
A laughing northerly and biting southerly,
The creaking wood that needs caulking,
Sealing boards of their sulking.
Yesterday's tomorrow has yet to arrive
and harbour intentions with harmless playthings.
This beautiful life is yours for the keeping,

This beautiful life is mine for the taking.
Have we these thoughts together,
Or are we separate like the sea and the sky?

Love without a bridge between earth and stars.

Us

W. F. Stubbs

Someday we'll cross these oceans
And sight will be no barrier,
And we'll meet upon this land
Where itchy feet will carry us.

These waves will have our back
And lap against our shoulders,
And the sun will burn tales
Into retinas of the older us.

Someday we'll hear magpies call
And seagulls will turn ever onward,
And we'll leave our bones on the shore
Where seeing will no longer bother us.

Pale

W. F. Stubbs

Te Reo translations by Sean Delany, Te Āwhina Marae o Motueka (2018)

To write. To pale the flow. To sentence the objective. To initiate the response.

All the words stacked in front of me. Paper. Print. Shelves.

An empty sorrow.

A hardened grief.

A never ending guilt.

~

She lays in front of me, green grass is white in the spaces I can't remember; sunglasses over eyes, glare of the sun reflecting off dark tints, hands over abdomen, mature breasts under a simple silk shirt low cut to her white collarbone and neck. The smile awaits my words, but my words are not there. Fingers in book's pages, pages silently spread across bulging calve muscles as eyes wander her three-quarter jeans, frayed ends over nimble knees. Her feet pedal the air in casual canvas shoes waiting for lost words to be found, reshaped, to spill from my mouth.

But I like this moment too much, this silence, this appreciation of our togetherness. A light breeze catches her greying hair. I cough, she laughs—that chuckle of a long life of struggles and finding joy on the other side.

Are you an angel?

Perhaps. I like to stay pale and interesting.

Are all angels pale?

Don't be silly.

I'm pale and *un*interesting.

Her cheeks rise to the bottom rim of the sunglasses.

I didn't used to be. Pale that is (I've always been uninteresting). Well, at least where the sun gets to shine. My skin used to go temporarily golden in the hot sun of Tūranganui-a-Kiwa. No one mistook me for Māori though—my dark bushy eyebrows and hairy chest pointed the Italian out for everyone. Il Italiano peloso.

She chuckles again.

I want my lips to connect with hers but wonder if it is too soon to lean in.

Does she want me to lean in? I wonder what she is thinking.

What was it like?

Can't really complain. There were much more hairier Italians than me around Gizzy.

No, silly! I mean, what was Gisborne like? I heard there's a lot more cultural diversity.

I shrug my shoulders,   into

                    they float

emptiness.

Normal. Pākehā, Māori . . . during later – more recent—years Chinese, Indian, Turkish with their doner kebabs (oh man I love those things!

We share a shish kebab between us, fingers all over the skewered pork pieces dripping in pineapple juices. She is unaware this is not the version I prefer, but is super happy with our fingers touching. I am happy too.) all graced our airports just like, I guess, any other town or city. We can't go back now. Roads were paved, steel imported, buildings erected; cars now travel where legs used to.

Good legs.

I agree. Strong legs. There's a story of J.S. Bach walking 450 kilometres to hear an organist in Lübeck perform. 450 kilometres. That's a long way!

Those were the days. Before your kind flew?

Yes.

Many moons ago we flew too.

We've only ever had the one.

Sunlight squints down. I wish I had brought sunglasses. Colonisation has happened, the effects were felt. Western ideals defined poverty where there was none before, only mana and respect. When someone else's label defines you, that is the only definition they allow themselves to see you through.

I heard there were gangs.

There's gangs everywhere.

Hmmm. True. Her feet fidget, stroke each other. Anyway, are you going to read me something?

I smile. Sure.

~

I dream of solitude, peace and quiet. When I find peace and quiet I have no need to dream anymore.

I live, for the living is what I live for.

~

Summer is like a dream here. Torturous heat reduced to smudged impressions. I hear her voice, long distances away.

I have been to Lübeck—my other self lives there.

Germany? You like to travel.

Well, there wasn't much else to do. We came here to learn. Tāngata, āputa.

I feel like I am the one learning.

There is a shift, something forgotten; a darkness, a place of birth. Whenua.

Her people, her kind.

Ko ngā marama me ngā tai, koia ngā mea pūmau kua ngaro atu ki tua; nā te kāpura i kai i tea ao, i te pō—kua hoki rātou kit e pō-uriuri. He mea tauhou rātou kit e hikoi ki tuawhenua. Will you remember the water flows over us?

I think so.

A fall,
  from above.
    The river collap
                ses
                  and sends gushes of white foam
                                down upon our bones. A splashing veil, laughing echoes and bouncy smiles.

I am in heaven, surely.

You did not believe you died.

I have no alternative explanation.

One will arrive. It will sit, it will converse; sound will travel follicles, beat against eardrums, send signals; synapses will snap, crackle, and pop—as your kind say.

I wonder if breakfast is far away.

You hunger to tell me a story—is this true?

I think so. You lay on white grass with me, sunlight absorbing tinted sunglasses, silk shirt melting against your breasts. All my thoughts were eyes. There was a book too, but the words were useless.

You'll remember how the useless looked. It will come back to you.

I believe her of course. I wondered what she thought of my body.

It's attractive.

In what way?

I like how your shoulders are terse, polished skin outlining your joints and muscles. That vein travelling down your arm wants me to know how it feels, what it would be like for my fingers to caress it into the inner elbow and down the outer ulna. I like how your chest – yes, it's hairy – defines the slimness of your torso and gentle, oh so gentle, abdomen muscles meet the bones of your hips. Has no one ever told you how attractive your kind are?

Only the magazines. But they were always a different kind.

A light breeze catches her greying hair, attaches a few strands to her lips, momentarily. She has mastered the art of the flick and sends whispers back into the breeze.

Why grey?

It's not all grey.

No, but your age—fifty?

It seemed the least . . . threatening?

I don't think that's the right word, but I know what you mean. Trying to connect on an even plain, a plateau of understanding, would have been forced with anyone younger. I shy away all the time because I can't force myself on anyone. I don't have the personality for that.

This is a good trait. You'll be liked, you'll be loved.

I'll be forgotten.

And remembered for kindness.

This, what you and I have, feels natural.

We have a communication.

Is it like your other communications?

There is no answer.

,west coast rain pastelises the canvas..

Summer smudges inwards I trot along.

~

Caffeine has brought alternative satisfaction. Thickly beaten froth—when froth done right—slips between my lips. Tramlines and whistles ease the burden of a crumbled city being scaffolded back into the modern era.

There is still beauty here, in amongst overgrowth surrounding stone walls fenced off, the banging, the clanking, the sawing engines and voices, doors' locking clicks and slams of footsteps coming and going. Every waking hour, every waking minute, every lost second.

There is still beauty here. A warm and loving heart accompanies me.

But the heart I seek is elsewhere.

~

Green ferns do not cover her the way they cover others. She stands on no pāua shell with long hair hiding the same parts that the other fifty percent or so possess as well. (Her hair isn't long enough. Greyness retracts up to speckled shoulders.)

It's just a body.

I raise my hands to my hips, my penis stiffening. My right hand gestures towards her. It's definitely a body I like!

She smiles gorgeous blossoms at the intensity of my erection, the direct line leading down to testicles, slightly parted hairy legs, upwards to an intimate belly button.

Your kind! She splashes me.

Water is rain cascading down naked thighs, a crotch burning with desires. Falling froth crashes over scaffolded rocks, a crumbling will to stronger, stranger thoughts.

~

Birdsong! I forgot birdsong.

In my sleep. Birdsong is sleep.

The song . . .

the song it sleeps.

~

What is colonisation?

I am awake. It is when the other takes over the space of an indigenous.

We were selves taking over each other. We had nowhere else to go.

That's not the same. There is no respect for maintaining the integrity of the original dwellers. Colonisers are rarely sorry—maybe some of the offspring are, once the full extent of damage is seen, but the falsehood of politicians seeps through even when claims are made to the contrary.

I feel like I should be apologising.
This was mutual.
I colonised your thoughts.
You allowed me my dignity. I maintained integrity.
Maybe I'll go away.
I'll still be left in my original state.
You sound like you won't miss me.
Missing another is subjective.
Can I come and visit?

There will always be a grass for you to lie down on, a sun to glare off your tinted glasses, a book for my fingers to open and eyes to ignore, words to be forgotten.

Words to be reshaped from the lost,
she says.

You

Jashan Kaur

We've been here since last winter.
Yet it feels like lifetimes ago
since I last felt the bitter winds on my face,
Nights and days blended into an everlasting haze
What I have gained and what I have lost, all to You?

Then there are those days, the worst days.
I can almost feel it, your iron fingers loosening their grasp.
The unending rain, so near I can smell it
Will your shadow finally leave my walls, will You?

You let me, let me climb.
I climb like a man desperate for sweet air in his lungs.
Scrape my knees, on the way to the boundless lands
but you always win, don't You?

Your rain drowns me, your sun burns me.
The higher I climb the further I fall, yet you aren't satisfied.
You embed your eternal marks onto my soul
Why do I stare at me and all I see is You?

The seasons fly as I drop pieces of me running away from you.
What's left I plaster onto walls, write onto notes,
scream to the world,
Desperate to leave a mark; to last
until all I have of me is You.

The Grey Above

Dan Witters

Down in Osborne City the sun would probably have been above the horizon and shining at a low angle through the waves at Waikare Beach; but up in the Ngarere Hills the rising sun was mostly blocked off and all we got was a very faint lessening of the night as my Dad and I climbed up the big hill behind the farmhouse on Tiwhiri Station. The farm belonged to my mother's sister Maddy and her husband Robert and I'd spent a lot of my childhood walking up to the summit. I liked stopping off at the dams on the way up and the view from the top of the hill was great. It was the highest point for miles around and from the lookout you could see all the way back to Osborne.

The Maori word 'Tiwhiri' means 'digging up something that's been covered over' and it can also mean 'shining a light on something'. All the farms around Osborne seem to have Maori names. No one ever changes the name of a piece of land when they buy it. Apparently, it's bad luck to do that. I don't know why it got called Tiwhiri. What was covered up? On winter mornings there's usually grey mist over the hills and all the way down the valley to the schoolhouse, so perhaps that's it. I asked Uncle Robert once, but he said he didn't know. It was just called that when he bought it.

Actually, I'm not sure he did buy it. He was in the New Zealand army in the war and when the soldiers got home, the ones who wanted to be farmers put their names into a ballot and the lucky ones got sheep farming land. I suppose they had to buy the sheep. Anyway, I've got a bit side-tracked, because what I want to tell you about is me and my Dad going duck shooting and what happened. The day started when Dad came into my cousin Jane's room where I was sleeping and wakened me very quietly. I was surprised to find I'd been to sleep at all. I was so excited at the prospect of being taken shooting that I'd thought I was never going to get to sleep, but I must have drifted off. Jane didn't wake up when I got out of the bed next to hers.

It would have been about five o'clock, but I don't know for sure because like most kids, I didn't have a watch. I got dressed and went out into the hallway and down to the kitchen, right at the end. It was a big farm kitchen with a faded blue, wooden table up against one wall on which Dad had put out some things for breakfast. He was having porridge, but he knew I hated porridge. Mum would have made me eat it if she'd been there. She was pretty strict about that sort of stuff, but Dad always used to indulge me when she wasn't around.

I was probably a bit spoiled by Dad. He was older than most of the other fathers. He was fifty-four years old. He'd been too old to go to the war in 1940. All his brothers and all the men who'd married his sisters had gone to North Africa and Italy. Dad hadn't been scarred by war. I had some toast and a bowl of Golden Queen peaches. I got them out of an Agee preserving jar using a serving spoon, which Mum would have been pleased to see and then I ate them with a dessert spoon so that I wouldn't be licking the spoon that went back into the jar. Breakfast only took a few minutes and we didn't really wash up. Dad just rinsed our plates in the sink, and I followed him out the back door to the car to get the shotguns out of the boot.

Dad had a grey and white Austin A55. Cars like that were called two-toners. There was a line that ran horizontally around the car from the bottom of the windscreen and across the doors just below the windows, where the two colours met. The top half was grey, and the underneath was white. We got out our gumboots and put them on. Everyone in New Zealand had gumboots. One of our teachers told me that they were called gumboots because the men who worked in the Northland forests digging out kauri gum used to wear them. I don't know if that's true, but it sounds right, and it makes sense. However, someone else told me that they started out in South Africa and that they were originally called gommeboots.

I often find there are two versions of things and you can't be sure which one's right. My Dad had two shotguns. A big one and a little one. I can't remember what the big one was. It had a name like Browning, or Remington, or something like that. But I remember the little one. It was a Churchill. It had been hand-made for some English gentleman and my grandfather had bought it from him before coming back from the First World War. It was several inches shorter than most shotguns and quite a bit lighter.

My Dad said it would be perfect for me. He'd spent about half-an-hour out on the tennis court the night before, teaching me how to handle a gun. He'd showed me how to break the gun and load both barrels; how to walk with the gun broken; how to cock it; and how to aim. Squeeze the trigger gently, don't pull at it. He told me about creeping up on ponds where the decoys had been set; why you had to shoot above the target when you were shooting uphill; what to expect when the ducks flew off and the difference between Paradise, Mallards and Greys and the way that each behaved. There was a lot about gun safety, safety catches and never getting in front of the other hunter's gun.

My Dad was wearing a big, loose-fitting, checked shirt that only had three buttons coming down from the neck and you had to pull it over your head to get it on. The checks were green and brown and dark colours, so it was okay for hunting in. No bright reds to give us away, although I suppose it will turn out that ducks are colour blind and that he could have worn a bright red shirt for all that it mattered. We went through the wooden gate by the shepherd's hut and across the cow paddock over to the corner where the giant puriri tree shades the ground and no grass grows.

I had to watch where I was walking so as not to step into a cow pat. Martha, the milking cow, had left the end result of her ruminations pretty well everywhere in the paddock. If you'd asked me what a cow was, I would have told you it was a ruminating quadruped. I was pretty bright for an eleven-year-old and I had no trouble remembering words. I even knew a word to describe myself perfectly. I was precocious. Uncle Robert put me onto that. I would have found that definition of cows in a quiz book. We didn't have television in 1961; well, some parts of the country might have, but not the provincial farming town where I lived. So, in the evenings, to keep everyone amused, Uncle Robert and Aunty Maddy would ask us questions from quiz books. Quizzes were very popular at the time. There was one broadcast on 2XG each week and we'd all sit around the radio trying to beat the contestants to answer when the compère asked the questions.

We climbed the fence in the corner of the cow paddock, under the shade of the puriri tree. Well, strictly speaking, seeing the sun wasn't up yet there probably wasn't much shade to speak of. We broke the barrels of our shotguns even though they didn't have any cartridges in them. Dad said you had to practice your safety drills all the time so they'd become second nature to you. We climbed over the wire fence, holding the large wooden corner post that the runs of wire were stapled onto. Then we were in the Hill Paddock.

All the paddocks on these sorts of sheep farms had names. Not very inventive ones—the Back Paddock, the High Paddock, the Willow Paddock, Glen's Run, the River Field. It's as though when people came to some subjects back then they really played it safe with names. We seemed to have lost that Old Testament enthusiasm where God brought all the animals to Adam to name and he dug into his memory and came up with giraffe, hippopotamus, iguana, mastodon and so on.

Look, I know Adam didn't think up those names really. I mean, he probably spoke Hebrew, so he wouldn't have known enough Greek to come up with hippopotamus. And anyway, even God hadn't thought up Greeks back then. But what I wonder about more is whether Adam actually had a memory at that stage. It's only a couple of chapters into Genesis and Adam is getting on pretty well with his Dad and is doing all this naming for him. Not much has happened, apart from everything being created, and Adam hasn't got to the bit where he gets to know the difference between good and evil. These are pretty innocent days.

So, did he have a memory to get the names out of? Perhaps he just made a noise like 'Gimel' (that's the Hebrew word for a camel) and God said, "Well done boy, we'll call that weird humpty thing I just made, a Gimel." It's a kind of neat little father and son story. My Dad wasn't quite such an easy-going parent as God, so he did most of the naming for me. "This is called the stock, this is the barrel, this is the trigger and this very important little lever here is called the safety catch. Whenever you're walking with a gun, you leave it on, whether the gun is loaded or not."

Lucky Adam if he didn't have a memory back then. Later on, as he and the family trudged east from Eden, he had plenty to regret. Although, it's not the things you do that cause you problems.

They're always over in an instant. It's the fact that you have to live with them. The fact that you can remember them. Even that might be okay, if it were constant; but memory has this other trick that allows us to hide bits we don't like. I suppose if we didn't, we would probably just go mad; but we don't really hide them, they fester away in the bottom of our minds and change the way we do things. They're like nasty reverse puppeteers hiding below the surface of our life, pulling strings and making us do and say things differently from the way we really want to.

The Hill Paddock gets steep and so we walked along the fence line. This meant we could keep our guns either crocked in our left hands, or over our shoulders, and pull ourselves up, holding the wires of the fence with our right hands. You can't hold the top wire because it's barbed. I've never been sure why, and I didn't want to display my ignorance by asking one of my uncles, or even worse, one of my cousins. "What do you mean you don't know what the barbed wire's for, you townie?" they'd be bound to say. I suppose it's something to do with keeping stock from jumping the fence.

The Hill Paddock reaches a plateau and there's a level piece about a hundred yards long before it climbs again to the first dam, which was our destination this morning. We'd been up there in the afternoon the day before and had set the decoys on the dam. We stopped once we reached the flat bit and loaded our shotguns. Dad put the cartridges in and stepped back, nodding to me to close the gun. I reached under the barrels, put my hand on the wooden fore-end, clicked the gun shut and checked the safety catch. I felt a surge of something that was probably a mixture of pride and excitement. Going shooting with your Dad for the first time was an important thing for boys my age. I felt that this was a moment I would never forget, no matter how many times I went hunting.

We walked on and I kept a few yards behind my father. He had a grey woollen balaclava folded up so it covered the top of his head and his ears. He wasn't a tall man, but he was broad and strong, and he had never seemed as wonderful as he did then, walking calmly and purposefully ahead of me towards the dam. We were almost silent, except for the soft swish of our gumboots through the grass and the occasional scraping noise as we brushed against the bulrushes dotted through the paddock.

The safety catch is on the right-hand side of the Churchill, just above the trigger. It makes a very faint click when you push it on or off. From a few yards in front of me my father wouldn't have heard me clicking it. If he had, he would have been very annoyed because you never play with the safety catch on a loaded gun. He would have been annoyed as well because he would have said I was fiddling. He didn't often get angry with me, but he often used to say, "Stop fiddling, boy." It was something he couldn't stand.

We got to the far edge of the flat area and approached the fence. It had six strands of plain number-eight fencing wire and a seventh strand of barbed wire. I can remember it clearly, in perfect detail. We got to the fence together. Dad was about to climb over, using the fence post for support, but he noticed that I was on his left and starting to climb in the middle of the run between two posts. You don't do that. The wire sags under your weight and you haven't got a post for support. You never do that. He took his foot off the first wire and moved to the other side of the post and gestured to me to move to the right and to use the post. Neither of us had broken our guns. What madness had descended upon us? Nelson Blake, the most careful and meticulous man I ever knew, failed to take the simplest of safety precautions. Perhaps it was just destiny that prevented him.

Anyway, that was the last communication between me and my Dad. He signalled to me to move to the right and get some support. My ears rang and my vision blurred. Dad slumped against the fence and just ahead of us a flight of ducks took off from the dam and flapped into the sky sending warning calls to each other. The shotgun blast went straight up into his throat and pretty much took his head off. My Dad and I never really got to go duck shooting.

Wish upon a Star

Hannah Ruelens

Wish upon a star. Wish upon a falling star. Children are the only ones to actually believe it works, and yet so many people wish anyway. Not really believing, but hoping nonetheless. When in a desperate situation or just wishing for more, people look at the stars, marvel at the vastness of space and hope that maybe, someone out there is listening. Of course, even if there is someone listening, that still doesn't mean that they will intervene or do anything to help. But for the purposes of this story, imagine that they do. They hear your plea and intervene. What then? Will you even know they intervened or just believe you did it yourself? Do you ever thank the stars, if your wish has been fulfilled? You should. Because whoever is listening in on us and is powerful enough to intervene on your behalf can definitely also intervene to destroy your life. And they are sick of their thankless work. So now, when they hear a wish, they ignore it, or, if they're feeling really malicious, make sure the situation gets worse. The most creative of them sometimes fulfil the wish, but make sure you regret the fulfilment immensely. Sayings don't appear out of nowhere, after all, and 'be careful what you wish for' is no exception.

Sometimes, however, sometimes they have pity. Sometimes they hear a wish, hear the desperation and hopelessness in a voice, and have mercy. And they fulfil their wish. A small push here, a fortuitous occurrence there. And they hope. They think; maybe this one is different. Maybe this time, we'll be thanked. But they never are. It's therefore no surprise that they seldom fulfil wishes now.

But what about the children? I hear you say. Surely small children show thankfulness for wishes fulfilled. Surely, they believe in the impossible. And you're right, children often get their wishes fulfilled. They're too small to understand that people don't wish and actually expect something to happen. And, just like they've been taught by their parents, they say thank you after receiving a gift. But it eventually ends. Eventually, small children grow up and learn that they work for their successes and that wishes are fulfilled by other people. And they stop wishing on the stars and believing it will work. They join the masses that forgot the magic in the world. They assume those wishes were fulfilled by parents or friends or their own imaginations, instead of the stars. And so, a constant cycle is established, where the wishes of children are fulfilled and with thanks rewarded, until they learn to wish on other things and no longer believe, which leads to moving on to new children. It might sound banal to you, fulfilling the wish of a child. Don't they only think about the new toys, what could they wish for that's not one of those? What you forget is the reason behind the requests for toys. To play. To let their imaginations run wild. And no-one is as imaginative as a child. Wishes for an adventure with a dinosaur. Flying through the air on a Pegasus. Saving the world from an evil plot. Nothing is too much, too creative for them to provide. And with such creativity abounding, why would children want to leave?

You don't. You, like some other children, grew up and lost the belief in wish-fulfilling stars, but still long for that freedom of expression, those impossible visions vaguely remembered. You go looking for just one more taste. Bright colours, the fur of a unicorn under your fingers and the sound of its neigh in your ears. Only, it feels too short, too small a peak at something you once had. So, you indulge again. And again. It gets harder to sleep without something to dull the loneliness, you become afraid of not being able to go back. Back to that place of smiles and happiness. So what if you shut out your friends, your family. So, what if your work suffers, so what if you no longer remember parts of your day. It's not important. Just focus on the freedom, the glimpse of something you missed so much. It's not the same, but it's the closest you're going to get. Sometimes, your brain rebels. It tells you that it's not real. That it's been fun, but you're needed in the real world now. That's ok, you just need to take a larger dose. A few more sips of that wonderful brew. And maybe some more. Your brain gets more powerful, but so do you. Just inhale some more. And more. Until one day, you permanently join the world you so desperately wanted to find again. And that's perfectly fine with you.

Above, the stars shine brightly in the sky.

It All Happened

(lyrics)

Sarah Holliday Pocock

He gives me his big smile and stats about his game.
My questions sail across the sky wild and overthrown.
Because the thoughts I have on this sport are? a dried up well.

But I say I love you and I mean it.
But I say I love you and cricket's incomprehensible.
I say I love you and I mean it.
Does that count for something?

She's fourteen and I have to be invisible.
She says I called her name and she almost died.
The distance between us can feel like a canyon.

But I say I love you and I mean it.
I'm proud of you everyday — or almost everyday.
I want everyone to know you're mine.
Does that count for something?

You say, are you going to put that milk away?
You say, do we really need all these jars?
My projects stretch to the sky like the redwoods.

But I count my blessings that you like me still.
I say I love our life and also these jars.
I say I love our life to the end.
Does that count for something?

There may have been a younger me.
Who stayed up too late.
Who knew everything.
But who knows if that ever really happened.

But I say I love you and I won't forget.
But I say I love you and it all happened.
I say I love our life until the end.
Does that count for something?

About the Authors

My dad ***Rodney Taina Baker***, a member of the Tairāwhiti Technology Trust Hub writers group, passed away early in 2022. Dad wrote about World War II, the war my grandfather, his dad, fought in. That's why his poem in this book is *The Italian Campaign*. Dad was, all-round, one cool guy, man and friend. He worked hard and played hard all his life. He loved a good guitar singalong with friends and family, with anyone that wanted to jam, laugh and tell stories with him. My dad Rodney had not a bad word to say about anyone. He would, literally, give you the shirt off his back. He loved sports, especially golf. Boy, he could show Tiger a thing or two! A Manurewa supporter for many years, dad also loved rugby. I reckon he would have been a hearty All Blacks coach. My dad loved my mum, me and his mokopuna so much. He has gone now to live among the stars, where he looks down upon us with love and best wishes. I have really appreciated this opportunity to sing his praises. Naku iti noa, John Baker.

Aaron Compton is a writer of fiction and poetry, with a fair few stories and poems out there in various media across Australasia including: paper, digital, film, paint, marker pen, literary journals, recited from stages, and on one occasion yelled from a bartop. A lover of microphones—onstage or in studio—recently he's been dabbling in audio. He has co-edited two anthologies: volume one of *Kaituhi*

Rāwhiti (woohoo!) and *Te Korero Ahi Ka*, an anthology of New Zealand speculative fiction, which won the Sir Julius Vogel award for best collection. He's worked in various parts of the cultural sector, including seven years as a museum educator, first at Te Papa Tongarewa | Museum of New Zealand, then at Tairāwhiti Museum. Aaron has also worked in theatre, galleries, and had some memorable times as an artist assistant. Aside from the audio his degree in digital film rarely gets used—it was mostly the screenwriting aspect which interested him; his teaching qualifications haven't been dusted off for a while, either. Aaron lives with his family in Tūranganui-a-Kiwa where he whistles, in tune. He is from Rangitāne and Ngati Kahungunu ki Wairarapa.

Writing began as blogging for ***Vicki J Cosson***, to document the family sailing adventure; updating friends and family on their progress, being sailing newbies: @thepurplepirateship.blogspot.com From their exploits, Vicki landed a couple of paid articles in the Caribbean sailor's magazine, All At Sea. Having homeschooled the three boys, she recognized the need for more fun, informative, non-fiction books for kids. So arose "Eden Lives On A Pirate Ship." It's whimsical, rhyming, filled with piratical and nautical terms; ending with a sea shanty and glossary and shows what "a day in the life" looks like, living on a boat-- see:https://books2read.com/edenlives-onapirateship. Vicki has since been crewing with local waka hourua, Tairāwhiti, doing day sails, voyages, and harbour visits. She also is the creator of Seaglass bags, made from upcycled sails and materials, with 10% of all proceeds funding sailing adventures for foster teens.

Tahui Pare Ihimaera Crawford, nee Smiler or Polly, was born in Gisborne on the eighteenth of August 1948. Her parents are Tom and Julia Smiler from Whanau a Kai and Ngati Ira descent. Her childhood memories are of a loving relationship with siblings and her parents who she credits for all her achievements. She was employed by the National Bank in Gisborne in 1970. During her career she transferred to branches throughout the North Island. She retired in 2000 as a Commercial Manager in Gisborne. Polly also played Representative Senior Woman's Hockey for Poverty Bay, Hawkes Bay and *W*ellington. She married Barney Crawford in 1968 and they have three Adult children: Caroline, Vicki, and Haami.

Whanaupani Matemate Crawford, or Barnz, was born 19 June 1950. He is Maori, married and has three adult children. His Parents Apirana and Hariata Crawford lived in a rural settlement called Mangatuna just past Tolaga Bay. This is where he spent his youth and where a lot of his stories are set. He joined the Taitech Creative Writing Group in 2020, and with help of Katrina Reedy he started writing seriously. He is gifted with an excellent memory and he loves sharing memories of his youth in particular his Mum and brother Sam who passed away in 1967. Sam was his Lone Ranger—his Hero.

Originally from England, ***Dorothy Fletcher*** has lived in both hemispheres of this Earth, and has filled many roles in her life - from taking the curl out of wallpaper, to teaching and acting as the principal of a primary school, to being a wife, mother, grand-mother and great-grandmother. Throughout her years as a teacher, Dorothy used storytelling as a teaching tool. Gradually, some of those stories were written down. Now she writes novels for both children and adults, along with audience participation plays, which explore mayhem and murder, with a little humour thrown in.

Holly Flyger was born in Gisborne and has lived in Gisborne for seventeen years, with her family. Holly is currently going to

Gisborne Girls' High School where she is planning to complete her NCEA qualifications.

Janine Hamilton-Kells first discovered a love of writing whilst working as a volunteer biography writer for Hospice patients. Through this work Janine found that there is no such thing as an ordinary life, and if you have a passion or a crazy dream, then there is no better time than today, to pursue it. Janine is currently at the polishing end of a quirky romance novel with a speculative twist. Her second work in progress details the unexpected, tense, and often funny relationship between two different women thrown together through a surreal experience. When Janine isn't writing, she is sharing her love of dancing with others in the Rhythm n' Lines Linedancing club. Read about and visit her at: https://www.janinehamiltonkells.com/

Tēnei au, te hokai nei o taku tapuae. Nei rā ngā kohinga whakaaro, ngā puna kupu e whakamanatia ana e ***Cassiopeia Harrison*** mo ngā tūpuna i tū ki te mura o te ahi. E kawe nei e ia i te mauri o Hikurangi maunga, o Waiapu awa, o ngā karangatanga maha o te rohe mai i Rahuimanuka ki Mataahu. Ko Kahuitara, ko Pohatukura ngā tūrangawaewae. E whakapono ana e ia kia "kohikohia ngā purapura i mahue ake e kui mā, e koro mā hei karauna ki te ao." Koianei nā te whakamanatanga o tēnā. He puritia ki te reo me ngā hītori o Ngati Porou, hei aha, hei hoa haere mo tōna orangatonutanga.

Puri Hauiti is a teacher at Gisborne Intermediate. Both his parents were born and raised on the East Coast. His father was raised in Te Araroa, his mother in Whareponga, and he and his wife have two sons, Duke and Maia. Puri's Kuia brought him up in a whanau of storytellers, and Puri would sit, listen and be inspired. He bases his short stories on relationships with his Mum and mokopuna – each a journey of self-discovery and self-healing. After losing his mother to cancer, he aspires to inspire others who have lost a loved one to keep their legacy alive.

Charlie Holland (Te Aitanga a Mahaki, Ngati Porou) is primarily a short fiction writer, but also likes to dabble in script writing. A member of the Tairāwhiti Writers' Hub and NZSA, Charlie has become a passionate learner and listener of local histories and local storytellers.

Moana Hoogland is eighteen years old, and goes to the Gisborne Teen Writers Hub at the H.B. Williams Memorial Library. She has been published multiple times since age 13. Moana has loved writing since she was little, and her friend and she are currently working on a series, *The Infernian Chronicles*. Writing comes in many forms, and she finds the ability to express herself through poetry, stories and writing/making music is fun, calm and enjoyable.

Benita H. Kape was born in the Rangitikei and lived most of her life in Tūranganui-a-kiwi. Her work has been published online in *Poetry Shelf, Simply Haiku, Haibun Today, Lynx* and in *nzepc Fugacity 05 and Oban 06* etc. as well as in print in *The Gisborne Herald, Broadsheet, New Women's Fiction 3, Manifesto Aotearoa 101 Political Poems,* in *Kokako (*a New Zealand journal dedication to Japanese short forms), and in the *NZ Poetry Shelf Blog* owned by Paula *Green.*

Jashan Kaur is a 17 year old student at Gisborne Girls' High School. Jashan's interests include reading, dancing and 70's era music. She is very passionate about gardening and helping the environment. She also enjoys learning and hopes to study physics and botany at the University of Otago. Jashan takes inspiration from the world around her and the experiences she's had to write her poetry.

Jessica Keast resides in Tūranganui-a-Kiwa with her husband and three daughters. Jessica is a film publicist, working in the industry for 14 years, and is now studying marketing, film and communications. Creative writing is a beloved hobby that Jessica strives to make more time for and hopes to keep progressing with.

Taranga Kent is a teacher, author/poet/songwriter, small business owner (Kids Creation Stationz-Arty Farty School Holiday Programme) and community volunteer. For a long time she wrote for pure enjoyment on scraps of paper with no intention of them ever being seen by anyone else. Taranga moved to Gisborne 5 years ago to be near her mokopuna and found that she had more disposable time than usual. She discovered the Tairāwhiti Writers' Hub, and found the positive feedback received from other members very encouraging. Taranga has since realised that her passion in life is writing. She is excited at the prospect of seeing her work published for the very first time.

Norman Maclean has lived in Gisborne much of his life and has enthusiastically written fiction since childhood. He has had several short stories broadcast on Radio New Zealand's National programme, has written articles for magazines and published two books of non-fiction but continues to pursue his preferred field of fictional writing. The novel, *Revelation,* will soon be put online through Plaisted Publishing and will be available on Barnes and Noble, Amazon and Smashwords. It was subsequently published as a paperback in the United States, sold well through Muir's Books and after extensive revision is going to reappear early next year under a new publisher for distribution in the States as well as in New Zealand and elsewhere. Given the writer's numerous visits to the Mediterranean region, it is not surprising that the novel is an historical work set there and reflects the writer's fascination with classical civilisations and the emergence of Christianity as a radical new force in the Ist C.E. His short story, *Streams of Thought*, appeared in the first *Kaituhi Rāwhiti* collection of poetry and prose and was praised by Witi Ihimaera, who was a fellow student at Gisborne Boys' High school in the early 1960's.

Tērā ia e mā mai rā , e pākia mai e ngā ngaru o te moana. Ko te kurī -a-paoa. Kei ngā repo o te wherowhero te waka o horouta e takoto ana. Ko matiti te taumata tirotiro a Tāmanuhiri . He kōrero tēnei nā ***Te Paea Parengaio Maurirere***. He uri ia nō Te Tairāwhiti whānui engari, kei te Muriwai tōna ngākau e noho ana. She has always had a profound love for reading, and says that her love for writing sprung from there. "The way someone's words can be more than words has always been a skill I've wanted to perfect."

Ko ***Daphne Maxwell*** taku ingoa, Ko Hikurangi te maunga, Ko Waiapu te awa, Ko Ngati Porou te Iwi, Ko Tūranganui a Kiwa taku whare kainga, Ko Toowoomba, Australia te wāhi e noho ana ahau. Daphne Maxwell was born and raised in Gisborne. She moved to Australia with her husband, Chris, and their four children in May of 1995. The past 9 years they lived in Toowoomba. Daphne joined the Kaiti Hub Writing Group in September 2021. Being a part of the group has inspired her to write, which is something that she'd never really done up until then.

Christopher McMaster is currently working on his seventh novel, a romance set in the depths of time and space. His debut novel, American Dreamer is part of a series of three published by Dreaming Big Publications, and released in August, 2020. This year has seen the publication of his novel, *Pirates Come Down*, set in the fisheries of the near future, *MisStep*, an interstellar drug deal gone very wrong, and its sequel, *Seeders*. He has authored two collections of stories (*Journey to the Stars* and *On an Island Surrounded by Water*), and has written and edited nine academic books—however, he finds much more pleasure in making stuff up. Visit him at: https://christophermcmaster.com/

Phyllis McGann writes as Philomena and spent many happy years in Gisborne. She and husband Roger fell in love with its beauty, the people, the magic. Sadly, family drew them away to the East of England but they will return and Philomena is comforted by the privilege of being included in this anthology as a Tairāwhiti writer.

Arieal Sage Middleton was born and raised in Gisborne, New Zealand. Many memories by the sea, she is a lover of the ocean and of the green scenery. She has always been interested in the written word, through the influence of movies, books, and music she has taken an interest in expressing herself through literature. 'Waves at Bliss' will be her first published piece of writing and hopefully not her last. Sage works mainly with creative writing, either songs, poems or short stories. Many experiences have led her to where she writes today, and she looks forward to experiencing new adventures to benefit herself and her writing. An attendee of Gisborne Girls' High School, she plans to further her knowledge and career in creative writing.

Aimee Milne is a former registered nurse turned activist and writer who lives in Tairāwhiti with her husband, teenager, cats, dogs and chooks. She is completing a postgraduate diploma in creative writing through Massey University and is known for her anti-misinformation and anti-racism mahi. Aimee's writing has been published in *Newsroom, Stuff, The Gisborne Herald* and online literary magazines.

Gillian Moon is a writer, poet, editor, mother, and grandmother who has lived locally for many moons. She finds peace and inspiration at the city's beaches and has had some of the deepest and most memorable conversations with people she has met there, often while picking up rubbish or collecting sea glass.

Claire Morgan was born of British parents in 1951 in Germany and raised in England. Her interest in drama, dance and spiritual development led her to the work of Rudolf Steiner. She trained in Eurythmy. While in Switzerland she met her German husband, married and their daughter Sonia was born in 1980. They emigrated first to America, then to New Zealand. Claire enjoys contact with her brother in Scotland, her daughter and grown-up granddaughter in Hawkes Bay. Now retired in Gisborne, Claire and her new partner Rex, their Spaniel, Marcus explore this beautiful East Cape travelling in their fifth wheeler.

Karen Morris-Denby (Kaz): 'I have attempted every form of creative writing,' Kaz says. 'Some successful, some not. But I always return to my passion - writing for film.' Kaz's latest publication, *'Seaside Solitude'*, reflects her love of the visual and echoes her passion for photography and poetry. 'Chasing the light with music' is how Kaz describes her work. She says, 'you just have to watch and listen and find the miracles.' All her writing is for the spoken word. Kaz has a Diploma in Drama. She has always been eager to perfect her craft and has attended numerous writing workshops in Australasia.

Vanessa Ngarimu lives in Ruatorea and is the mother of five beautiful children. She was born in Kawerau; Mum was from Taranaki, and her father a Nati. The whanau relocated to the East Coast when Vanessa was a teenager. A staunch rugby fan, coach and player, with a background in martial arts, Vanessa was always artistic, and recently started an art business – Black Lamb Creations BLC. She wrote Tapping Out while working on writing with school children. Vanessa's first published work is a brave high-impact story about the pain of losing a loved one to suicide.

Paddy Noble is a writer, blogger and Anglican Priest. Much of Paddy's writing is identity-based topics. He writes about being Gay and Maori and his life influenced and inspired living in Cambodia for twenty-five years. Paddy's genre of writing is theology, spirituality, science fiction, gay fiction using biblical themes, and screenwriting. To help Paddy spurn his writing ideas and concepts is his passion for blogging and creating online content. Currently, Paddy is working on a new blogging project that entails rebranding and strategising how he hopes to help and inspire others to blog around their interests and goals.

Ko Titirangi te Maunga, Ko Uawa te Awa, Ko Ruakapanga te Whare, Ko Te Aitanga a Hauiti te Iwi, Ko ***Molly Pardoe*** ahau. Molly is a member of Tai Tech Writers Group. She has submitted to the 'Voices from the Kaiti Hub' series. Her first love is writing poetry. However, she now enjoys writing short stories and has started penning her memoirs as a legacy for her family. "Well," she says, "that's the plan!"

Susan Partington is originally from the United States, but has called Tairāwhiti home since 2010. Her passion for the written word has recently led her to earn a diploma in Library and Information Studies. Susan enjoys both acting and writing for the stage. She won "Best Play" twice in the Tairāwhiti 48-Hour Play Festival, and is currently writing a full length play. Because writing is often a solitary pursuit, Susan enjoys the rich experience of playwriting and collaborating with other artists as they breathe life into the characters and stories.

Suzanne Pinfold was born in Whangarei, where she lived until her late teens before travelling around Australia and New Zealand. Settling in Hamilton, she raised two daughters, then after thirty years, moved to Auckland. Now happily retired, she calls Gisborne home. For Suzanne, writing is a receptacle for her imagination, a helpful way to clarify thoughts and mould ideas, and an important emotional outlet. Many years worth of exercise and notebooks attest to this. Her mission is to tell the stories of her family and childhood and compile her writing into books as a legacy for future generations.

Sarah Pocock moved to Gisborne from the United States in 2012 and within months realised how lucky she was to have found this beautiful community. This is the first song she's written. She works in the non-profit sector and makes music with a local band. Writing her novel, gardening, and crocheting are just a few of her many unfinished projects. She lives in Gisborne with her husband and two teenagers.

Ko ***Katrina Reedy*** awau. No Ngāti Porou, Te Aitanga a Māhaki, Kaitahu me Tainui ōku whakapapa. Ko Wi Pewh tōku hoa rangatira, kei Tūranganui-a-Kiwa māua e noho ana. Ko Mere-Rohi rāua ko Morgan a māua tamariki. Ko Harper, ko Jade me Wolfe a māua mokopuna, ko aku tamariki mokopuna nga mea nui o tōku ao. I ēnei tau tae ki te mutunga o 2022 he akonga pakeke awau i whiwhi Tohu Paerua o te Mātauranga mai i Te Kunenga ki Pūrehuroa. E toru aku pōtae mahi inaianei. Tuatahi, he kaitohutohu mātauranga mo tētahi kamupene. Tuarua, he kaiwhakaako tuhi auaha awau i taku hāpori. Tuatoru, he kaipatopātuhi awau mō tē rōpū whakatika ataata whai muri i te hui ā-tau mō Treaty Based Futures 2022. A muri nei, ko taku hiahia i te ao tuhituhi ko te whakaputa i taku pukapuka tuatahi o taku raupapa 'Literary Active - guided poetry writing journal for all seasons'.

Hannah Ruelens is an eighteen year old, whose family moved to Gisborne from Belgium four years ago. She enjoys both reading and writing fantasy. Lately, she's been experimenting with writing romance, but somehow always ends up with horror, which her submitted piece is an example of.

Lien Ruelens is from Belgium, and moved to New Zealand in 2018 when she was 10 years old. *Whispers* was inspired by a variety of different sources, mainly from her love of creepy love stories and her infatuation with the character, 'The Blood God'.

Roman Seaton is a passionate, albeit unprofessional scribbler; he is a resident hobbyist writer and artist at Campion College. His first publication, inspired by the atrocities that were the 1960s moors-murders, was encouraged extensively by his parents & mentor, which he considers as the tipping-point in his aspirations for writing. Since then, he has tinkered and tapped away at his own full-length fiction-piece. His latest entry, *Golden Calves on Silver Screens*, draws influence from his own experiences within the near cultic underworld of tv-personality and its pseudo-religious idolozations of the "ideal life".

Beverley Smith attended Primary School at Tuai and High School in Gisborne. After her O.E. it was always at the back of her mind that one day she would return to Tairāwhiti, which she did in 2003. A highlight of her working life was employment as a cook in a Swiss Finishing School. Airline work also gave her opportunities for many wonderful travel experiences. Beverley attended Writing Courses with the late Gordon McLauchlan and the late Hilda Phillips – President of PEN and extra-mural literature studies at Massey. She is an Accredited Lay Preacher of the Presbyterian Church of New Zealand and Funeral Celebrant.

Elise Smith is an award winning author, certified writer, blogger and writing coach. Elise has written and published her autobiography trilogy, "The New Zealand Dream series" by Sheila (pen name.) Elise writes to inspire and give hope to others. Elise has published "Johnathan," co-authored with her late father, a memoir about growing up in Manchester England during the war. Elise writes in fiction, non-fiction, poetry and content. Elise runs a successful blog with seven writers contributing, she has published many articles, interviews, short stories and guest posted on sites. Visit her at: https://www.mynzdreamblog.com; Instagram: #mynewzealanddream

Victoria (Torri) Stewart is a poet, gardener, artist and lover of books. She moved to Tairāwhiti in 2017 and has been proud to be able to put down roots here and call it home. Her time is stretched between running her home for two children, a small poodle and her husband; working for a Hawke's Bay based digital marketing agency; and spending as much time as she can in the garden. Torri writes poems on a range of subjects as inspiration takes her, usually reflections on life and the world around her.

Warwick (W F) Stubbs has written two novels, *I am the local Atheist* and *Auralye on a Harp*, a book of poetry, *The Tasman Journey*, and is currently working on a third novel and two more books of poetry. He has been a songwriter, guitarist/vocalist in a prog-rock heavy metal band, and has composed orchestral and chamber music. After leaving Campion College Warwick worked for a year at Rainbow Fast Foods before moving to Auckland where he eventually worked as a book buyer for Highland Park Paper Plus. In 2003 Warwick moved to Invercargill, receiving a Bachelor in Contemporary Music from SIT in 2007, and went on to begin a 6-year stint of teaching. He currently resides in Paekakariki.

Dan Witters grew up in Gisborne and attended Kaiti, Wainui and Ilminster Schools. After leaving university he worked in Gisborne for 10 years as a lawyer. He moved to France in 2003 and lived in Bordeaux. Wrote 2 novels that were published as eBooks, *Cubespace and The Grey Above,* both available online. Dan was script editor for several television series, including *The Legacy of China.* He has worked as an editor for a range of writers based in Europe and Africa from 2003 – 2014. Dan is presently writing a novel called, *The Carrington Effect*, about a post-apocalyptic Gisborne and writing short stories for a collection he hopes to publish in 2022. Dan has been living in Gisborne for five years since returning from overseas in 2016 and plans to continue living here and writing.

R de Wolf is a Māori author, poet, editor, and Indie Publisher from the East Coast - *Ngati Porou, Te Whānau-ā-Apanui, Ngai Tahu, Ngāti Mutunga.* She lived overseas for 29 years and lives in Tūranganui-a-Kiwa - Gisborne. Publishing her debut Pacific fiction novel, *Guardians of the Ancestors - Book 1* of the six-part *Spirit Voyager Series*, and short-story *Crushed Violet*, in *Kaituhi Rāwhiti* in 2020, 2021 saw the release of *The Future Weavers - Book 2* and

Poetry in a Pear Tree. In 2022, the dystopian novel *The Goodness Algorithm* was launched, with *Poetry In a Pohutukawa* and *Brothers in Whalesong* due for a summer release. R de Wolf is also a volunteer tutor at Tai Tech. Find out more at www.rdewolf.com

ACKNOWLEDGEMENT & GRATITUDE

It takes a mighty team effort to build an anthology. The writers and their words are the stars of these pages. They created the constellation that Witi witnessed rising over the horizon.

Katrina Reedy kindly volunteered her time as the Te Reo Māori editing consultant. Thanks to Poet and Editor Aaron Compton for contributing his awesome proofreading skills - cheers mate.

Award-winning photographer John Flatt of 'Lightseeker Photography' *(johndflatt@gmail.com)* and the internationally renowned weaver of the Michelle Hinekura Kerr Collection *(IG michelle-hinekura FB Michelle Hinekura Kerr - Kairāranga Artist)* and graphic designer Ezra Whittaker-Powley *(ezrawhittakerpowley@gmail.com)*, donated their artistic work and valuable time to support the writers. We cannot thank you all enough.

The original *Kaituhi Rāwhiti,* (before we had numbers), was made possible by a generous grant from the Margaret King Spencer Writers Encouragement Trust. Due to the success and sales of the first anthology, we were able to partially fund the printing of Kaituhi Rāwhiti Two, and many thanks to the NZSA Central District Committee for the funding support for the launch. Accolades to our local bookstores, Paper Plus, Muirs, Ballance Street Bookshop, the Tairāwhiti Museum, Witi Ihimaera, and Monty Soutar for their awesome reviews and the many readers who purchased copies, supporting the talented writers of Te Tairāwhiti.

KAITUHI RĀWHITI ONE

A celebration of East Coast Writers

If you enjoyed Kaituhi Rāwhiti Two, then you'll want to see where it all began!

"It's like hanging out with a group of Coasties enjoying a barbecue at the beach. We've just had a feed from the grill of sausages and kai moana, cooked to perfection by the four editors, our glasses have been filled with either beer or wine (well, for the adults), and now it's time to break out the guitar and sing some songs.

These contributors each sing a mean waiata,"

--Witi Ihimaera

An anthology bringing together the imagination, memories, story and verse of thirty-three local writers from the Tairāwhiti.

From up the coast to the depths of space, from the horrific to the poetic, there's something inside for every reader.

www.ingramcontent.com/pod-product-compliance
Lightning Source LLC
Chambersburg PA
CBHW070543120726
47909CB00007B/2223
9780473630331